Drew H

ESSAYS

WRITERS SERIES 26
SERIES EDITORS:
ANTONIO D'ALFONSO AND JOSEPH PIVATO

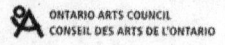

Guernica Editions Inc. acknowledges the support of
the Canada Council for the Arts.
Guernica Editions Inc. acknowledges the support of
the Ontario Arts Council.

Drew Hayden Taylor

ESSAYS ON HIS WORKS

EDITED BY ROBERT NUNN

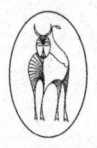

GUERNICA
TORONTO — BUFFALO — LANCASTER (U.K.)
2008

Copyright © 2008, by Robert Nunn, the Authors,
and Guernica Editions Inc.
All rights reserved. The use of any part of this publication, reproduced,
transmitted in any form or by any means, electronic, mechanical,
photocopying, recording or otherwise stored in a retrieval system, without the
prior consent of the publisher is an infringement of the copyright law.

Robert Nunn, editor
Guernica Editions Inc.
P.O. Box 117, Station P, Toronto (ON), Canada M5S 2S6
2250 Military Road, Tonawanda, N.Y. 14150-6000 U.S.A.

Distributors:
University of Toronto Press Distribution,
5201 Dufferin Street, Toronto (ON), Canada M3H 5T8
Gazelle Book Services, White Cross Mills, High Town,
Lancaster LA1 4XS U.K.
Independent Publishers Group,
814 N. Franklin Street, Chicago, Il. 60610 U.S.A.

First edition.
Printed in Canada.

Legal Deposit – Second Quarter
National Library of Canada
Library of Congress Catalog Card Number: 2008928099
Library and Archives Canada Cataloguing in Publication
Drew Hayden Taylor : essays on his works / edited by Robert Nunn.
— 1st ed.
(Writers series ; 26)
ISBN 978-1-55071-268-1
1. Taylor, Drew Hayden, 1962- —Criticism and interpretation.
I. Nunn, Robert, 1939- II. Series: Writers series (Toronto, Ont.) ; 26
PS8589.A885Z63 2008   C812'.54   C2008-902879-1

Contents

Acknowledgements	6
Introduction by Robert Nunn	7
"How Native is Native if You're Native?": Deconstructions of Authenticity in Drew Hayden Taylor's Performative Project by Birgit Däwes	17
Drew Hayden Taylor's *alterNatives*: Dishing the Dirt by Robert Nunn	59
From Copper Woman to Grey Owl to the alterNative Warrior: Exploring Voice and the Need to Connect by Jonathan R. Dewar	77
The Spiritual Tourist in the Plays of Drew Hayden Taylor by Kristina Fagan	124
Your Hand Weighs Exactly One Pound: Misrecognition and "Indian Humour" in Drew Hayden Taylor's *Blue-Eyed Ojibway* Series by Rob Appleford	149
Introduction to *Girl Who Loved Her Horses* by Ric Knowles and Monique Mojica	183
Interview with Drew Hayden Taylor by Birgit Däwes and Robert Nunn	190
Biography of Drew Hayden Taylor	241
Bibliography	244
Contributors	253

Acknowledgements

Birgit Däwes. "An Interview with Drew Hayden Taylor." *Contemporary Literature* 44.1 (Spring 2003), 1-18. Excerpts reproduced with the permission of the author.

Jonathan R. Dewar. "From Copper Woman to Grey Owl to the alterNative Warrior: Exploring Voice and the Need to Connect." *(Ad)dressing Our Words: Aboriginal Perspectives on Aboriginal Literatures*. Ed. Armand Garnet Ruffo. Penticton: Theytus, 2001. 57-77. Reproduced with the permission of the author.

Ric Knowles and Monique Mojica. "Introduction to Girl Who Loved Her Horses." *Staging Coyote's Dream: An Anthology of First Nations Drama in English*. Ed. Monique Mojica and Ric Knowles. Toronto: Playwrights Canada, 2003. 313-14. Reproduced with the permission of the publisher.

Robert Nunn. "Drew Hayden Taylor's alterNatives: Dishing the Dirt." *Crucible of Cultures: Anglophone Drama at the Dawn of a New Millennium*. Ed. Marc Maufort and Franca Bellarsi. Brussels: P.I.E.-Peter Lang, 2002: 209-217. Reproduced with the permission of the publisher.

Drew Hayden Taylor, dir. *Redskins, Tricksters and Puppy Stew*. Videocassette. National Film Board of Canada, 2000. Excerpts reproduced with the permission of the National Film Board of Canada.

Introduction

ROBERT NUNN

Several years ago, at a conference in Brussels, I read a paper on Drew Hayden Taylor's *alterNatives* to a roomful of people, including the author. I prefaced the paper by saying that I felt self-conscious talking about his play in his presence: not in the sense of feeling socially awkward, but in the sense of being face to face with the question, *What do you think you're doing?* I said that there were several possible answers to the question regarding the function of criticism: a very long answer, a long answer, a short answer, and a very short answer. The very short answer had the advantage of being plainly and simply true: this stuff was fun to talk about.

I think all the contributors to this collection would concur. Taylor's plays are fun to see, all his writings are fun to read – and everything he writes is fun to think and write about. Certainly, as you will see, they are great fun to quote.

So that is where we start. But where we find ourselves going deepens the experience immensely. For Taylor's works raise insistent questions, often catching the audience or reader off guard and provoking painful and difficult reflection. For starters, we are faced with the collision of assumptions in the very term "Native humorist." How do assumptions about the celebratory nature of humour gibe with the history of five hundred years of oppression of Native peoples at the hands of Canada's white settlers? What happens when these collide, as they frequently do in his plays? The problematic relation between Native and white gives an edge to Taylor's humour. The range of tone is great, from anger at the history of oppression and the racist and triumphalist assumptions that have driven it, to amused frustration at the questions Native people get asked by non-Natives, to gentle mockery of another category of white stereotyping, the appetite for easily digestible tidbits of Native spirituality. Then there are the conflicting assumptions about the very meaning of the word "Native," not only assumptions by the predominantly white culture about Aboriginality – assumptions steeped in the orthodoxies of colonialism – but also the conflicting ideas and attitudes within the Aboriginal communities themselves, around such problematics as mixed blood, the virtual disappearance of many Native languages, and the cultural hybridity of most Native people. As a person of mixed ancestry, Ojibway on his mother's side, Caucasian on his father's side, able to understand but not speak his mother tongue, bearing a name that "is not a proud Aboriginal name my great-great-great grandfathers would have understood or appreciated" (*Futile* 13), with those emblematic blue eyes, Taylor himself returns to the vexed question of identity again and again. In "What's in a Name?" (*Futile* 14-15). Taylor proposes wonderful new names for ethnically hybrid Native people, starting of course with a reference to his own earlier manifesto as the founder of a new nation, part Ojibway, part Caucasian, hence *Occasion,* "or, as I frequently have been known to think of myself, a Special Occasion" (Futile 14). His most recent play, *In a World Created by a Drunken God* (2004), turns the joke down a much darker path. In it, a mixed-blood man, who has never known his Caucasian father, is visited by his white half-brother, who has tracked him down to make a request: the father is dying, and only a kidney transplant can save him. The father has only revealed the existence of the Native half-brother in the hope that he might be persuaded to donate a kidney. Is he willing to be tested to see if he is compatible? For the mixed-blood character, it comes down to an agonizing recognition: is he willing to view himself as a stock of body parts kept in reserve for the Caucasian half of his parentage?

Several essays in this collection address the question of Native identity. Jonathan Dewar, writing as a person of mixed blood, proposes a troubling affinity between mixed-blood and imposture. My own essay examines the demolition of simplistic white notions of Native identity in Taylor's alterNatives. Birgit Däwes argues that Taylor's plays propose a Native identity that is not an essential core of self but a performative construction, experimental, playful, unstable and changeable.

Three of the contributors to this book (Dewar, Fagan, and Mojica) are mixed-blood, like Taylor himself. The others are non-Natives; and the shadow of cultural appropriation hovers over any activity such as theirs. How does a non-Native critic discuss work by a Native writer without purporting to stand in his place and explain what he is all about? As Appleford points out, no matter how attuned a white scholar may think he/she is to Native culture, he/she is not able not to benefit from the relatively privileged position that goes along with being white. As Bruce Cockburn's song goes, this is a stolen land. On top of that, there is the point Ojibway scholar Kimberly Blaeser has made: that "the insistence on reading Native literature by way of Western literary theory clearly violates its integrity and performs a new act of colonization and conquest" (55). In the essays that follow, certain Western literary theories are indeed made use of. Theories of ideology and interpellation, for example, proposed by the French critic Louis Althusser, figure in Rob Appleford's essay. Several of the essays in this book, including mine, apply postcolonial theory to Taylor's works. It produces, I think, productive readings, but not without problems. As you will see in the interview, Taylor agrees with Thomas King that the "post" in "postcolonial" obscures the truth that for most Aboriginal people in Canada, colonization has not ceased.

A further problem for non-Native academics writing about Native literature is our eagerness to jump on a term made prominent in the first place by Native writers, and, sometimes with rather unseemly eagerness, hunt for its traces everywhere. I refer of course to the Trickster. Native Earth Performing Arts' *Trickster's Cabaret,* the centrality of trickster characters in Tomson Highway's *The Rez Sisters* and *Dry Lips Oughta Move to Kapuskasing,* and Highway's own assertion in the preface to *The Rez Sisters* that the Trickster is "as pivotal and important a figure in the Native world as Christ is in the realm of Christian mythology" (xii), plus many other evidences of trickster imagery in Native literature and art, have sent many a non-Native academic on an enthusiastic trickster hunt. Daniel David Moses has mockingly referred to this as "the spot the trickster syndrome." Whether or not contributors to this volume are guilty of turning a genuine insight about an aspect of Native culture into a cliché, is something you will have to judge for yourself.

Still, there is one thing that white scholars can legitimately do when examining Native literature, and that is to concentrate on what Terry Goldie calls "the image of the Indigene" and Daniel Francis "the imaginary Indian." Rather than purporting to interpret Native cultural production, the white scholar can examine her/his own cultural biases in the act of reading Native texts. He or she can ask: what images of the Indigene has our culture constructed; are we reading these images into the text; is the text interrogating these images? I don't know how typical my experience is, but in reading Taylor's works, I haven't learned nearly as much about Native identity as I have about the identities manufactured by my own culture and imposed on Native peoples. Thus in my essay I examine how in Taylor's play *alterNatives,* certain key concepts of Aboriginal identity, produced in the first place by the white colonists, are forced to disclose their latent content. Rob Appleford focuses on the role of the non-Aboriginal listener, in the economy of "Indian humour." He discusses how non-Native readers of Taylor's humourous articles can misrecognize themselves as the targets of friendly teasing, thus imagining an acceptance into the circle of Aboriginal life that is not at all real. Addressing the same issue of the "image of the Indigene" from an Aboriginal perspective, Kristina Fagan examines the humour directed at the non-

Native "wannabe" – the spiritual tourist – and argues that the joke does not necessarily leave the joker unscathed.

So far this introduction has focussed attention on the many facets of Taylor's humour. But there is another dimension to his work that demands acknowledgement. As Ric Knowles and Monique Mojica argue in their introduction to *Girl Who Loved Her Horses,* a play for young audiences, and Taylor's favourite out of everything he has written, that dimension is what they term "the numinous." It may seem a little far-fetched to compare Drew Hayden Taylor to El Greco, but bear with me. When I saw an exhibition of El Greco's paintings at the National Gallery in London, England, in 2004, it was a revelation. I had always assumed that all his art was distorted and expressionistic. But half the paintings were painstakingly realistic. They were portraits of real people, and his painting style captured everyday reality. The other, non-realistic paintings were of spiritual subjects, and he was painting a different order of reality in a very different style. Something like that is the case with Taylor. His plays for adults – the comedies and dramas – portray everyday reality, the humour comes from his sharp-eyed observation of daily life, and the style is realistic. When, on the other hand, Taylor writes plays for young audiences, their realistic surface is disturbed by another order of reality, which makes its presence felt through expressionistic distortion. *Toronto at Dreamer's Rock* is set at a place of power, site of vision quests for generations. Its power draws together Native teenagers from the past, the present and the future. In *Boy in a Treehouse,* a mixed-blood boy being raised by his widowed father, who is white, attempts to undertake a vision quest in his backyard treehouse. He receives guidance from a girl his age, whose name and uncanny ability to walk along thin tree branches hint that she may be the spirit of his dead mother. And *Girl Who Loved Her Horses* departs even more radically from everyday reality, as it shifts from realistic dialogue to dance. It would be good to see a fuller exploration of the spiritual dimension of his work than can be found in this volume.

The complex issues of both substance and style that I have outlined above are provocative and challenging to address. But I return to my starting point. Drew Hayden Taylor's plays and other writings are fun: fun to see, fun to read, fun to think and write about. And here I would like to recall what Brecht wrote in *A Short Organum for the Theatre:*

> From the first it has been the theatre's business to entertain people, as it also has of all the other arts. It is this business which always gives it its peculiar dignity; it needs no other passport than fun, but this it has got to have. (180)

Works Cited

Blaeser, Kimberly. "Native Literature: Seeking a Critical Center." *Looking at the Words of Our People: First Nations Analysis of Literature*. Ed. Jeannette Armstrong. Penticton: Theytus, 1993. 51-62.

Brecht, Bertolt. *Brecht on Theatre*. Ed. and trans. John Willett. New York: Hill and Wang, 1964.

Francis, Daniel. *The Imaginary Indian: The Image of the Indian in Canadian Culture*. Vancouver: Arsenal Pulp, 1992.

Goldie, Terry. *Fear and Temptation: The Image of the Indigene in Canadian, Australian, and New Zealand Literatures*. Kingston: McGill-Queen's University Press, 1989.

Highway. Tomson. *The Rez Sisters*. Saskatoon: Fifth House, 1988.

Taylor, Drew Hayden. *Futile Observations of a Blue-Eyed Ojibway: Funny, You Don't Look Like One, # 4*. Penticton: Theytus, 2004.

"How Native is Native If You're Native?"

Deconstructions of Authenticity in Drew Hayden Taylor's Performative Project

BIRGIT DÄWES

1. Native Theatre: A Silenced Genre

Native or First Nations theatre is not only the oldest but also the one most silenced and misrepresented literary genre of North America.[1] Ever since N. Scott Momaday's Pulitzer Prize for *House Made of Dawn* triggered the so-called "Native American Renaissance" in 1968, Native literature has almost exclusively been associated with the genres of fiction, autobiography, and, to a lesser extent, poetry. Native theatre, on the other hand, is commonly displaced into the field of ritual drama, pertaining to a long lost past, and as such is usually relegated, if at all, to the academic interest of anthropology or religious studies. While some 180 plays by Native playwrights had been published by 2003, and eight anthologies over the past twenty years have been exclusively dedicated to Native theatre, the critical canon as well as the market have widely failed to acknowledge this literary movement.

Most fortunately, this development is currently changing. Especially in Canada, where the influential Native Earth Performing Arts Theatre Group was founded in 1982 and where, in 1986, Tomson Highway's *Rez Sisters* "marked the watershed for the coming onslaught of Native plays" (Taylor, "Canoeing the Rivers" 25). Native theatre has been receiving notable national and international acclaim.[2] As Drew Hayden Taylor puts it,

> [i]f in 1986 there was one working Native playwright in all of Canada, today at least three dozen playwrights of aboriginal descent are being produced and published. If that rate of increase continues, by the year 2020 it is conceivable that everybody in Canada will be a Native playwright (Taylor, "Alive and Well" 256).

With this increasing presence and reception of Native theatre, critical questions surrounding its definitions and categorizations follow into the foreground of the project of "Creating a Dialogue to Talk about Native American Plays," in Diane Glancy's words (143). As is apparent from these discussions, the elements central to Native theatre – aside from questions about the genre's formal classification – crystallize as the issues of identity, its cultural construction, and its mediation.

2. "All the World's a Stage?" Performative Identity Politics and the Dangers of Essentialism

The relevance of identity construction has always been crucial in Native American literature. Ever since colonial times, constructs of "Nativeness" have been instrumentalized and appropriated for profit and power, and the unbroken demand of anachronistic or pan-tribal stereotypes today – which has been termed "Indianthusiasm" by Harmut Lutz (see Lutz 15) – dangerously feeds on notions of authenticity.[3] Cherokee director Elizabeth Theobald regrets such colonialist expectations especially in regard to Native theatre: "Native playwrights are writing about powerful women, family crises, adoption, and cultural alienation. The wider public wants Geronimo, Cochise, and Black Elk" (142). On the other hand, and sometimes in response to this form of cultural oppression, essentialist approaches with particular emphasis on origin and biological heritage are also still present and popular, and not necessarily in Gayatri Spivak's sense as "strategic essentialism" (3). Helmbrecht Breinig offers the diagnosis that Native people "keep returning to the question of an integrative group identity with great persistence. Tribal vs. pan-Indian, rural vs. urban, reservation vs. off-reservation, conservative vs. modern, or even postmodern forms of existence are being negotiated" ("Introduction" 24). In times of open borderlines, crumbling concepts of "nation" or "culture," and increasingly vigorous forces of "political correctness," this is, as historian Arthur Schlesinger explains, an understandable move: "The more people feel themselves adrift in a vast, impersonal, anonymous sea, the more desperately they swim toward any familiar, intelligible, protective life-raft; the more they crave a politics of identity" (12). In this quest for certainties, however, the argumentative logic used especially in response to acts of terrorism in the U.S.A., the Middle East, and Europe, clearly illustrates the dangers that essentialist, fixed notions of identity – regardless of which national or ethnic entity they are applied to – globally pose to democratic ideals of dialogue, peaceful coexistence, and human rights. The trauma of 9/11, its consequences of limited civil rights in the United States (see Chomsky 126), George W. Bush's 2002 postulation of the "axis of evil," and its results for the "enemies" in Afghanistan or Iraq (see Bush n. pag.) are primary cases in point. With these recent global developments in mind, the search for new, differentiated identity politics in dialogic process crystallizes as highly topical and in constant need of renegotiation.

In an attempt to substitute the ontological foundation of identity by a dynamic, and polysemous process, David Hollinger has argued in his *Postethnic America* that human beings usually choose to be part of various (even conflicting) social groups at the same time and therefore, instead of being identified, voluntarily and revocably perform their notions of self as "affiliations" (see Hollinger 6-13; 105-11). Identity, deduced from Hollinger, is not an ontological but a functional term; it is the site of confluence of the personal and the political, decisively shaped by discursive and performative agency. For this reason, questions of representation are inseparable from questions of identity. That this is particularly relevant for the silenced genre of Native theatre is underlined by the fact that of the 72 entries listed under the Library of Congress's subject heading "Indians of North America – Drama" only 13 (18%) are actually plays by Native Americans or publications about them.[4] The largest number, however, is constituted by so-called "Indian plays," those colonialist and usually racist theatrical works in which America's Native population is (re)presented through the lens of the cultural majority, a practice that manifests what Linda Alcoff has termed "speaking for others": "a desire for mastery, to privilege oneself as the one who more correctly understands the truth about another's situation [which leads to] erasure and a reinscription of sexual, national, and other kinds of hierarchies" (29). Therefore, whether one represents oneself or is represented by someone else makes all the difference, and the stage as the forum of negotiating "performative" identities turns out to be more than a metaphor.

As an analysis of three plays by Ojibway dramatist Drew Hayden Taylor will show, Native theatre provides powerful alternatives to conventional politics of identity. In *Toronto at Dreamer's Rock* (1989), *alterNatives* (1999) and *The Buz'Gem Blues* (2002), Taylor employs trickster-like playfulness, humour, and — as Robert Nunn has convincingly shown in an application of Homi Bhabha's theory — postcolonial mimicry (see Nunn, "Hybridity" 109-16) — to undermine the logic of essentialist identities, deconstruct notions of authenticity, and to cleverly subvert processes of representation. Identity (in its prominent sense of signifying ontological substance) is exposed as the site of inter- as well as intracultural oppression, exclusion, and appropriation, which is in dire need of revision. Drew Hayden Taylor eventually envisions a model of what Helmbrecht Breinig and Klaus Lösch call "transdifference": a blueprint for interculturalism in which difference is marked by "a simultaneity of — often conflicting — positions, loyalties, affiliations and participations" (Breinig and Lösch 21), and celebrated as dynamic, performative, always in-progress, and under constant discursive (re)construction.

3. Negotiations of Native Authenticity in Toronto at Dreamer's Rock

Toronto at Dreamer's Rock, first staged on October 3, 1989 at the Sheshegwaning Reserve on Manitoulin Island, Ontario, brings together three sixteen-year-old boys who share the same ethnic background (Odawa and Ojibway), but who come from three different points in time. Rusty, a contemporary teenager looking for a part-time refuge from familial difficulties and problems at school, climbs "Dreamer's Rock" – a place formerly used for vision quests and meditations – which now becomes the setting of a crack in what astronomers would call the "spacetime continuum." He is mysteriously (and involuntarily) joined by Keesic, who enters from a pre-contact past and is just as confused by the meeting as Rusty. The boys seem to have nothing in common, and although by "magic" (*T* 16) they suddenly speak the same language, their conflicts seem insurmountable. Just when Rusty has successfully marginalized Keesic as "primitive," the third protagonist, Michael, appears from 2095 and relativizes both of them. They all engage in a conversation about their tribes, tradition, personal problems, and survival, constantly trying to challenge each other's claims to their identities. In the beginning, their encounter is marked by power struggles, cynicism, and misunderstandings, but as the evening proceeds, they realize that they can valuably contribute to each others' lives if they adopt a larger perspective, acknowledge each person's right to speak for himself, and celebrate their differences as enriching. As Michael puts it, "[a]ll knowledge matters. In order for the mind to grow it must consume a variety of subjects" (*T* 52).

At first glance, each of these figures seems to represent a generalized (or "authentic") feature connected with his time: Keesic stands for the "true" Odawa tradition unspoiled by European contact; Rusty embodies a stereotypical idea of contemporary reserve life (marked by alcoholism, lack of future perspective, and poverty), and Michael is the icon of a future in which medical care has progressed but the environment is polluted and distinct features of Odawa culture have been lost. At a closer look, however, these clear-cut categories are exposed as discursive constructs commonly instrumentalized for domination.

In the course of overlapping personal and political power struggles, the figures experiment with various strategies of identity manifestation. When Keesic first appears, Rusty derives his claim to superiority from the place, stating that "I was here first" (*T* 19). This "anti-colonial" attempt to preserve his literal and psychological space not only resounds with historical irony, but remains ineffective: Keesic does not waive his right to be there. In a next step to keep his opponent and his "fortune-cookie talk" (*T* 20) at bay, Rusty names him, thus inscribing on him fixed labels of identity like "Tonto" (*T* 20), "Moses" (*T* 30), "Rip van McGregor" (*T* 27) or "Buckskin Bill" (*T* 34). He later tries the same strategy of categorization with Michael, labeling him "Flash Gordon" (*T* 34), "Sherlock" (*T* 51), "Obi-Michael-Kenobi" (*T* 52) or "Buck Rogers" (*T* 58). Similarly to Rusty (although a little more subtly), Michael also employs the strategy of categorization to dominate Keesic and Rusty. By assigning them to different inferior historical drawers, and turning them into objects of academic interest, he imitates the colonialist practice of many anthropologists: "I have a history teacher that would love a chance to interview subject matter like you" (*T* 34). Unlike Rusty (but like many missionaries and European-Canadian government officials), he does not show any overt rejection, but instead assumes the role of the well-meaning teacher. Not only does he interrupt or correct the others' statements (*T* 31, 51), but he also plays with his power to reveal or withhold information about Rusty's future.

Interestingly, in their power-oriented approaches, both Rusty and Michael undermine their own strategies by unconsciously revealing the instability of fixed icons of identity. When Michael is asked by Rusty who he is, for instance, he refrains from the "authentic" and acknowledges subjectivity's multiple dimensions: "Philosophically, psychologically, economically, culturally? Be specific" (*T* 33). And Rusty, too – although he seems to believe in biological origin as the source of a homogeneous identity – implicitly denies this same concept through his anachronistic name catalogue. In his attempt at identifying – and thus representing – Keesic as primitive, he adds connotations from the Bible ("Moses"), from American literature about Dutch settlers ("Rip van McGregor"), and from an assimilated form of Chinese food ("fortune-cookies"). For Michael, his reference to a nineteenth-century (again, fictional) European detective is arbitrarily mixed with allusions to *Star Wars* and two science-fiction comic heroes. However unaware Rusty may be of it, his use of such a variety of labels imparts that the identity that is authentically "Indian" to him is already heterogeneous, multicultural, and hybrid. Additionally, as Robert Nunn has convincingly shown with reference to Taylor's *Baby Blues* (1995), *Someday* (1991), and *Only Drunks and Children Tell the Truth* (1996), through this frequent use of elements from popular culture, "Taylor's plays do not just parody discourses of popular culture, they mimic them, in Bhabha's use of the term; they *interrogate* them" ("Hybridity" 116). In *Toronto at Dreamer's Rock,* references to *The Wizard of Oz*

(*T* 22), Charles Dickens' *A Christmas Carol* (*T* 35) and *The Bay City Rollers* (*T* 45) complement this point.

The notion of authenticity itself is most forcefully deconstructed by the characters' different definitions of "Nativeness." From the beginning, this concept is eroded by Keesic, who when asked what nation he belongs to simply replies, "We are the people" (*T* 38) or, logically from his point in history, does not even know what an "Indian" is (*T* 47). In a central scene toward the end of the play, the boys' biological, political, and even cultural criteria of validation have to crumble:

> MICHAEL: You know, in many ways, we're all very much alike.
> RUSTY: I hate to disappoint you there, Michael, but look at the three of us. We ain't nothing alike . . .
> MICHAEL: We're all Indians.
> KEESIC: I am Odawa, not this "Indian."
> MICHAEL: Okay then, we're all Odawa.
> KEESIC: No.
> MICHAEL: Pardon?
> KEESIC: No. I don't think you're Odawa. Or you, either. Everything I have heard today is not Odawa.
> RUSTY: Hey, I was born on the reserve. I am so Odawa and Ojibway. I got a card and everything.
> KEESIC: It's more than blood . . . Until our language is spoken again and rituals and ceremonies followed, then there are no more Odawa.
> MICHAEL: That's not fair. I know I'm Indian. Just because I don't like muskrat or moose meat is no reason to say I'm not Indian. (*T* 64-66)

While Rusty – in an ethnocentric line of argument – claims his identity with reference to biological essence and his accredited belonging to a political and national entity, Keesic represents a more indigenist point of view[5] by placing the language, the ceremonies, and the traditions at the center of Odawa identity. Michael, who would have the least claim according to both these standards, tries to transcend the conventional definitions by simply maintaining the right to perform his identity from what Hollinger would call a "postethnic perspective" (Hollinger 105). In addition, through their continually changing constellations and alliances, they reveal the dynamics of group formation as temporal and contextual, which convincingly undercuts any notion of communal authenticity.

Interestingly, unlike the others, Keesic does not try to overpower either the place or the people. Through his curiosity, he (literally) questions all the discursive patterns and hierarchies that the other two automatically accept. Thus, his openness turns out to be the key to overcoming the conflicts induced by their struggle for superiority and is the practical realization of Linda Alcoff's call for the right to speak for oneself. Catalyzed through Keesic, but achieved only through the cooperation of all three of them, the central proposition of the play is its celebration of dialogue. As Charles Taylor phrases it in "The Politics of Recognition":

> Thus my discovering my own identity doesn't mean that I work it out in isolation, but that I negotiate it through dialogue, partly overt, partly internal, with others. That is why the development of an ideal or inwardly generated identity gives a new importance to recognition. My own identity crucially depends on my dialogical relations with others (34).

Communication, according to this play, not only guarantees performative and open identity but is at the basis of any transdifferent approach. As long as these characters try to retain power and land claims through ideologies of essence, their conflict necessarily escalates in violence. However, when they perceive each other as human beings with similar experiences, they gradually accept each other's right to perform their own representation, which invites them to respect and understand difference as enriching; a perspective that Kathryn Shanley sees at the heart of Native American criticism: "Better many voices speak at once and we learn how to listen than allow only one voice to ventriloquize our own love song back to us" (697). That this achievement is not as easily gained as this play's closure may suggest has been illustrated by its sequel, *Toronto@Dreamer'sRock.com* in 1999, where the characters meet again twenty years later to renegotiate even more problematic positions (see Glaap, "Drew Hayden Taylor's Dramatic Career" 223).

Finally, as Drew Hayden Taylor chooses characters from within one ethnic group, his theatrical model of transdifference does not simply argue for intercultural understanding but questions the notion of ethnicity itself. Underlining that the central feature of identity and authenticity lies in their multiplicity of meaning, the play's entire political message is condensed in the polysemous title: The essence of the place "Dreamer's Rock" is neither just a concrete location in Ontario, a spiritual place of vision quests, a point of outlook, or a tourist attraction, but all of the above. Similarly, Toronto is not only a city in Canada (with all the associations of urban, mainstream life) but is a word whose etymology provides the key for understanding the entire play: in its original Odawa sense, Toronto means "where people gather to trade" or "any place where important things happen" (*T* 37) – an understanding that combines the temporally constructed meanings from past, present and future.

4. *Political Correctness and Trickster Discourse in alterNatives*

While in *Toronto at Dreamer's Rock* the gap between individual and communal identity is successfully negotiated through dialogue, openness, and respect, these methods largely fail in *alterNatives*. First produced on July 21, 1999 in Kincardine, Ontario, this play additionally brings all attempts at establishing authentic group affiliations to a clash. Angel, a twenty-four-year-old Ojibway science-fiction writer, and his partner Colleen Birk, a Jewish professor of Native Literature, are the hosts of a dinner party. Also invited are two other couples: Michelle, a "vegetarian veterinarian," and her partner Dale; and Bobby and Yvonne, a former friend and a former lover of Angel's, who are now a couple. In the discussions circling around identity, the personal and the political significantly overlap: relationship problems, personal insecurities and professional failures all fuel aggressions which are then acted out in a political field. As in *Toronto,* the need for fixed identities is instrumentalized for the establishment of social hierarchies, for which political labels are used as masks. In a step further than the former play, however, these labels go beyond Nativeness and cast a spotlight on the heterogeneity of "whiteness," including transnational denominators, such as Jewish or Celtic heritage, and, exploring the wider range of David Hollinger's "performative identities," even ingredients such as eating, drinking, or smoking habits, and professional or literary preferences. Reminiscent of Albee's *Who's Afraid of Virginia Woolf,* witty dialogues and sharp cynicism lead to an exorcism of politically correct labels, revealing their instrumentalization for discursive power and exposing the inherent dangers in their underlying layers of representation.

As in *Toronto at Dreamer's Rock,* the characters try to manifest their superiority over each other by various strategies. Colleen not only claims Angel as her property ("He's all mine, including his DNA" [*A* 32]) but tells him what to do, wear (*A* 10), read (*A* 37), write (*A* 16, 100), and even what to be. By trying to shape him into the writer of "the great Canadian aboriginal novel" (*A* 102), she tries to inscribe a Nativeness on him that fulfills her own expectations and may increase her prestige. Michelle, too, is dominant towards her partner; she openly shows her disrespect for Dale (*A* 32, 74) and forces him to be a vegetarian. Both women claim they only want to "broaden [their partners'] horizons" (*A* 37) – again a line ringing with historical and colonialist overtones of oppression. While these two women impose their desired "authenticity" upon others, Bobby uses this strategy for himself. Through a compulsive use of historical sarcasm, he continuously stages himself as a political victim and tries to gain credits of compensation by evoking guilt in others. His initial joke of having "to sign a treaty . . . to get a drink around here" (*A* 44) is met by an awkward silence, but despite this sanction he continues his game of breaking codes. When his provocative conflict with Michelle about vegetarianism escalates, and Michelle announces that she will go home, his cynicism culminates: "Home? To Europe?" (*A*

121). In perfect contrast to Bobby's separatism, Dale's strategy to maintain his position can be described as assimilationist. He does whatever is required of him, as long as it extinguishes differences and thus restores the harmony. All of these strategies are based on the belief in authenticity, and, via situational silences (which are effective methods of social sanctioning, see *A* 44, 63, 95, 99, 125), they lead to the breakdown of communication in the end: first Michelle, then Bobby and Yvonne, and finally Colleen resign from the dialogue by leaving the party in anger or bitterness. Dale joins Michelle out of solidarity but misses her and returns, so that the little hope for understanding that remains in the end is carried by the two characters who tried to evade the conflicts in the first place.

In the play's constructions of ethnic identity, semiotically speaking, the more elaborately the signifier of "authenticity" is articulated, the more it turns out to be floating, unstable, and *différant*. While "Nativeness" is initially defined by features such as oppression, extinction (*A* 37), profound spirituality (*A* 20), or more specific denominators such as eating moose meat (*A* 17), having an opinion on *Dances With Wolves* (*A* 47), or a good sense of direction (*A* 22), the icons of "Jewish" identity are assembled as knowing how to make rugelach (*A* 18), eating kosher meat (*A* 35), circumcision (*A* 36), or owning a menorah (*A* 112). Yet none of the figures fulfills expectations that match with his or her origin; on the contrary: according to these criteria, Angel fits more into the category of Jewishness while Colleen is certainly more Ojibway than anyone else. When Angel reveals that he likes science fiction, and Dale wants to categorize him as a "Trekker," his answer mocks both the affiliation to *Star Trek* and the notion of essential heritage: "Only half, on my mother's side" (*A* 94). Throughout the play, Angel makes use of the right to move outside the restrictions of protocol, shaping himself by references to other cultures (e.g. Chinese, *A* 98) or even staging himself as the European American frontier hero: "Oh oh, time to circle the wagons. The Indians are here" (*A* 40). In contrast, Bobby first establishes a clear role of authentic Nativeness (which he vaguely bases on the collective experience of "roaming this continent for 15,000 to 100,000 years," [*A* 119] or of presently being oppressed) and benefits from playing it. On the other hand, however, he contradicts his own tribalist performance, because, as chosen influences on his mindset, he lists a multicultural selection of Martha Stewart (*A* 41), Jean-Paul Sartre (*A* 48), and Friedrich Nietzsche (*A* 49) [6] – another good example of hybrid identities as constructed by a mixture of "high" and "low" culture (see Nunn, "Hybridity"

102-04). Eventually, Bobby even expresses the irrelevance of all labels by stating that "[i]t doesn't matter where the message came from as long as it's delivered" (*A* 50). However sharp Bobby's cynicism may be, it is Yvonne who most radically lays open the fissures in political correctness, because she writes a thesis about the inherent falsities of ethnocentric positions (*A* 76). Professionally proving that traditionalism itself relies on exclusion and selection and is thus an oppressive ideology, she severely criticizes the essentialism that often silences historical truths:

> In their hurry to recapture the old days of our Grandfathers and grandmothers, these people are being very selective about which traditions they choose to follow, often excluding many ancient practices that would not be considered politically correct in today's society . . . Centuries ago there were arranged marriages, frequent intertribal warfare, slavery, and in some cases, rumours of cannibalism. These are not even mentioned at Pow wows or Elder's conferences. It's as if they didn't exist. It's become a form of cultural hypocrisy (A 76).

What her arguments show is that authenticity is established on a very thin line between generalization and appropriation. Applying theories by Lewis Hyde or Paul Radin to foreground the idea of trickster-like "dirt-work" ("Taylor's *alter-Natives*" 210), Robert Nunn has argued that the severe "beating 'authenticity' takes in this play"

(213) serves as a "rite of passage" via the articulation of uncomfortable truths toward the insight that the "dirt thrown in [the characters'] faces" (210) serves an anti-colonial message: "the 'matter out of place' in this play is colonialism's byproduct" (215). The fact that Yvonne, who calls herself an "alterNative Warrior" (*A* 78), has been marginalized and excluded by her own community, casts a highly critical light on the policing and control of what can or cannot be spoken. This is additionally underlined beyond the fictional level by both the bomb threat Taylor received for *alterNatives* and the critical controversy surrounding the Vancouver productions of his *Sucker Falls* (a musical based on Brecht's *Rise and Fall of Mahagonny*) which arose because the latter revolves around "a corrupt Native person taking advantage of her people and the land claims procedure" (see Taylor, "Canoeing" 27-28). These textual and contextual instances of censorship perfectly exemplify that the dynamics of oppression and power work just as effectively within an ethnic community as they do transculturally.

In addition to these deconstructions of authenticity, *alterNatives* joins *Toronto at Dreamer's Rock* in advertising the semiotic openness that is needed for a transdifferent approach to inter- and intracultural understanding. Not only does the play's title already signify its multiplicity of meaning, but this level is strongly amplified through the humourous and playful language games of Bobby and Angel. When Michelle asks how Bobby and Yvonne got there (meaning Colleen's apartment), Bobby replies, "[a]ccording to rumours, across the Bering Land bridge" (*A* 58). Similarly, Angel frequently indulges in what is called "flouting conversational maxims" in pragmatics (see Grice 49), deliberately misunderstanding and evading questions as well as critically pointing them back at themselves:

> COLLEEN: Do you have a history with her?
> ANGEL: That's a difficult question to answer considering Native people tend to view history differently than non-Natives.
> COLLEEN: Stop these silly word games. I want to know if there's anything here I should worry about?
> ANGEL: Global warming? (*A* 91)

As all of this happens playfully and eventually serves the subversion of hierarchical concepts, both Bobby and Angel can be considered agents of what Gerald Vizenor has termed "trickster discourse": within the multi-voiced struggle of discourses which simulate authenticity, claim legitimacy, or even superiority, the "trickster sign" is the only one that exposes its own constructedness, wherefore trickster functions not only as simply a "language game" but as the primary mode of "shadow literature of liberation that enlivens tribal survivance" (Vizenor, "Ruins" 19, 13, 28, and *Manners* 77). By teasingly acknowledging that it is itself "a pose" without any representational claim, trickster discourse delegitimizes all such claims made by other (colonial or mainstream) literatures and puts an end to representational authority (see Vizenor, *Manners* 70). Quite significantly along these lines, the play's climax reveals that when Angel and Bobby were eleven, they were paid by anthropologists to tell them legends "as long as we promised they were authentic, handed down to us by our ancestors" (*A* 128). The stories they told were entirely made up, and they were published in a collection of *Legends of the Ontario Ojibway* (*A* 127), which is not only in its seventh printing but is also widely studied as "authentic" material at universities (*A* 129). Here, the instability of signification is ultimately laid open through a trickster sign which blurs the line between authenticity and fiction and thus points back to its own unreliability. To reinforce this effect, the end of the play underscores once more that all political debates on collective cultural identities eventually have to return to this basic semiotic disillusionment. When, in his final statement, Angel tells Dale a science-fiction story, he concludes by saying "The End" (*A* 144) – by which he marks the closure not only of the tale but also of the theatrical piece of which he is a part, thus reconfiguring himself and the audience in the larger fictionality that we like to think of as "reality." Much like in

Shakespeare's *Midsummer Night's Dream,* the ultimate permeability of the membrane between the authentic "truth" or "knowledge") and the invented ("fiction" or "dream") not only limits reality's only essence to its discursive constructedness but also points to the political consequences of this insight for authenticity-based identities.

5. *The Buz'Gem Blues* and the Limits of Identity Performance

Taking up the same issues that emerge from *alterNatives,* but less sharply and in the form of a comedy, Drew Hayden Taylor's latest play, *The Buz'Gem Blues,* which premiered at the Lighthouse Festival Theatre in Port Dover, Ontario on July 4, 2001, focuses on the role of authenticity in cultural appropriation and its academic representation as a form of censorship and control.[7] The setting – an Elders' conference at an unnamed Canadian university – brings together six characters of Ojibway, Cree, Mohawk, and European-Canadian (or "white") descent. As in Taylor's former comedies, the figures' relationships change in constellation (couples being separated and reformed) as well as in nature (familial, romantic, or professional), following patterns of romantic and domestic comedy in witty and humourous dialogues, which have gained the playwright the reputation of being "the Neil Simon of Native theater" (Glaap, "Margo Kane" 13). As in the two previously discussed plays, cultural identity is presented as non-essential and performative by personal choices. Its differentiation is reflected by three separate approaches to Native authenticity: While Martha, Amos, and Marianne represent the hybrid, postethnic stance, Summer stands for the "white" appropriator of Native identity whose figure casts a critical light on the freedom of choosing an affiliation, and *The Warrior Who Never Sleeps* illustrates the limits of Hollingerian performativity from an intra-cultural angle.

The first three continue Taylor's project of undermining Native authenticity through cultural hybridization, through their use of mimicry and popular culture, and through an overall ironic stance toward essentialism. Ojibway Elder Martha is highly suspicious of the conference, denoting herself as "a good Christian woman" who has "never been into all this sweetgrass-waving, tobacco-burning, walking-around-things-clockwise silliness" (*B* 13). Amos, the sixty-one-year-old lover of Summer, playfully approaches identity on the one hand by telling Martha that it is "very un-Indian" of her to drink tea without sugar (*B* 33), on the other hand by deriving his status from his outward appearance: "I'm an Elder. It comes with the beaded belt" (*B* 22). Both Martha's daughter Marianne, who prefers Tupperware to basket-weaving (*B* 50), and Amos, extensively indulge in cultural hybridity, which becomes obvious by their frequent references to American and European music ("The Judds of the Native community" [*B* 17], Red Foley [*B* 107], Céline Dion [*B* 65], the Beatles [B 108] and the Spice Girls [*B* 121]), television shows (*Gilligan's Island* [*B* 45]) or by the fact that they root their knowledge quite unhierarchically in Chatelaine magazine (*B* 13), Zen culture (*B* 107) or *The Oprah Winfrey Show* (*B* 115). All three of them additionally underline their postethnic affiliations through a playful exchange of prejudices between Mohawks, Ojibways and Cree (see *B* 71-73, 93), so that their ultimate belief in Hollingerian performative agency could be summed up by a credo of Martha's: "We have no control over who we are. But we have complete control over what we do" (*B* 41).

Apparently using the same belief, but from quite a different angle of the spectrum, Summer is a character in search of exactly the "aboriginal knowledge" (*B* 20) that the other three ironize. Being "one-sixty-fourth aboriginal" (*B* 21) and fluent in both Ojibway (*B* 39) and Cree (*B* 101), this white character is the perfect caricature of a phenomenon called "neo-Natives" by Paul Rathbun (108), "indians" [sic] or "autoposers" by Gerald Vizenor (*Fugitive Poses* 15), or "Indian impostors" by Klaus Lösch ("Cultural Identity" 69), i.e., persons of non-Native descent who appropriate a Native identity for purposes of profit, personal profile, or both.[8] Such appropriations of voice and identity have been classified as colonialist practices and as such have been extensively criticized by Native and non-Native writers alike. Ward Churchill, for instance, points out that this "birth of a new growth industry in the United States" started in the early 1970s and was initiated by non-Native people who adopted different names and identities in order to sell "Indian wisdom" in a more effective way (215, 217). Instead of criticizing Summer in an openly didactic way, however, Taylor simply has her ridicule herself through her appearance and interaction with the others. When she is introduced to Marianne for the first time, wearing enough necklaces, bracelets and rings to fit into "a Broadway musical" (*B* 66), her replies immediately reveal her strategy of instrumentalizing minority arguments for a personal pose:

> SUMMER: Do you dislike me?
> MARIANNE: Can I get to know you first?
> SUMMER: Do I look white to you?
> MARIANNE. Is this a trick question?
> SUMMER: Do you resent me for the way I look? Even though I too am a member of the great aboriginal nation?
> MARIANNE: Which nation? The Cleveland Indians?
>
> (*B* 53)

As in *alterNatives,* the line between political correctness and its absurdity is disclosed as thin and easily crossed. After finding out Summer's actual name, Agnes Ducharme, Marianne shows her that her quest is actually for herself, which she then engages in with as much naive eagerness as trying to be Native – until she meets The Warrior Who Never Sleeps.

This figure, described as "complete with dark shades, looking ultra-Indian" (*B* 16) is clearly her Native counterpart whose every utterance rings with heavy political overtones. Having "taken a vow that until our people are free, our customs respected, our culture honoured, I will be the Warrior Who Never Sleeps" (*B* 17), his identity has become collective in itself, embodying the political struggle of the Native minority in their resistance to both U.S. and Canadian governments. Slogan-like references to Leonard Peltier (a member of the American Indian Movement whose trial and conviction after the 1975 riots on the Pine Ridge reservation in South Dakota have been heatedly debated and have turned him into a symbol of the Native American struggle for rights), and Oka (the 1990 stand-off between a group of Mohawk people and the Canadian army over a traditional burial ground, see Däwes 8-9), underline the formulaic nature of his adopted collective stance. The reactions to his pose are highly interesting for the debate of identity politics, as – rather than subscribing to this "authentic" Cree's political struggle – all the other Native characters ridicule the Warrior: Marianne mocks his name as "The Warrior Who Likes Sheep" (*B* 62) or "The Warrior Who's Not Very Deep" (*B* 80; see also 48, 86); and Martha simply muses that "[w]hen I was his age, a lot of us wanted to look white. My, how things have changed" (*B* 33). When both women finally get him to talk about the self he tries to hide under his pose, he – like Summer – reveals his real name, Ted Cardinal. With this revelation (in which one's name, just as in *Toronto at Dreamer's Rock,* is affirmed as a valid token of identity) he opens up to tell them about the problems of his youth as a *Star Trek* fan and social outsider, finally seeing that his mask will not solve any personal problems. Marianne, who additionally mocks essentialism by breaking it down to an ultimately subjective level ("C'mon, find your inner Tedness" [*B* 88]), eventually summarizes the need for credibility: "I respect people for who they are. Sure I do. But is that who you are?" (*B* 81).

As all of the other characters refuse to take these two seriously in their chosen roles, Summer and the Warrior end up as evidence for the limits to David Hollinger's model of postethnic affiliation, which emerge from the interaction with a larger community: however performative and hybrid cultural identity may become, Ted Cardinal can as little pass for a warrior as Summer can pass for a Native. From this stance, *The Buz'Gem Blues* returns to Charles Taylor's thesis "that our identity is partly shaped by recognition or its absence, often by the misrecognition of others" ("The Politics of Recognition" 25); a recognition which – as in *Toronto at Dreamer's Rock* – can be negotiated through dialogue. Eventually, in an interesting double turn in the end, Drew Hayden Taylor has both characters first become their old selves again, then relapse into their roles together when they meet. When the Warrior accidentally erupts with "Free Leonard Peltier," Summer immediately responds with "Oka forever" (*B* 101), and their obvious connection is ironized only through the stage direction: "They both feel the magnetism. Pheromones are released. Somewhere off in the distance, a coyote howls" (*B* 103). Just when the figures' experiment with Hollinger's performativity is modified by Charles Taylor's principle of communal recognition, *The Buz'Gem Blues* goes on to deconstruct this theory as well: if recognition comes from one single other person (or another minority within a minority, such as the aboriginal *Star Trek* convention they finally elope to), it should be every individual's right to perform his or her poses all the same. Instead of dogma, Taylor offers humour: rather than exclude any Other by a specific intercultural theory, the trickster-like use of floating signifiers is probably the only strategy assuring cross-cultural openness, understanding and respect, as its irony encompasses every authority, especially that of the Self.

The third figure in *The Buz'Gem Blues*'s threefold approach to Nativeness is Professor Thomas Savage, a "white" anthropologist whose name already ironizes the historical icon of colonization that he stands for. Hoping to make use of the conference's participants for his research project – "[a]n In-depth Analysis of the Courting, Love, and Sexual Habits of the Contemporary First Nations People as perceived by Western Society. Volume One" (*B* 12), Savage is interested in obtaining and/or creating "a true representation of the culture" (*B* 24). Quite necessarily, this project has to fail: not only do all the Native characters he tries to interview turn around the hierarchy of analyst and research object, but they lay open the professor's personal problems instead, ridiculing his authority in the process. While Amos deconstructs Savage's role from a historico-political angle, responding "[s]aid the white man to the Indian" (*B* 26) to the Professor's affirmations of confidentiality and official legitimization, Marianne and Martha make fun of his superior attitude and undermine his professionality by repeatedly pointing out that his lack of relationships may seriously inhibit his common sense. When the Warrior sabotages his questions about identity through stereotypical phrasings ("That is what I am. That is who

I am. I have spoken" [*B* 58]), Savage reveals that his openness and alleged scholarly objectivity are actually subordinated to desired and preconceived results: "I don't want truth. I want information. Is that clear?" (*B* 59). In the end, the anagnorisis does not turn out to be the increase of knowledge he expected but, to the contrary, the insight that his methods had to fail. Finally admitting that "we now know less . . . than when the project began" (*B* 125), he shows his willingness to take the Native characters' advice of changing from an awkward, solitary theorist into someone more connected to reality, who really listens to what people have to say. Thus, at first glance, the professor seems to serve as a caricature with whose example the "white" authoritarian control over Native representation so commonly disguised as academic interest is successfully ridiculed and "talked back" to by the Natives. However, as a second glance – especially at the frame tale – reveals, the play does not simply rely on an anti-colonial reversal of roles. In Savage's prologue (a slide show reminiscent of Wendy Wasserstein's *Heidi Chronicles* which directly addresses and invites the audience into the play), as well as his concluding statement that leaves the audience to their own devices, this figure structurally takes on a similar function to that of Angel in *alterNatives:* mediating between audience and characters, Savage impersonates the trickster-sign that eventually exposes all discursive constructs as unstable and blurs the line between stage (fiction) and life (reality) – a tricked trickster looking "a little worse for wear" (*B* 125) maybe, but a trickster all the same.

On the level of representation, the three figures of Savage, Summer, and the Warrior elucidate the semiotic openness of authenticity from all possible angles. The colonial approach through a "white" academic lens is deprived of authority entirely. If Summer's new-age appropriation of traditional beliefs is also a colonialist act, the figure of the Warrior can be seen as its counterpart, impersonating extreme anti-colonial resistance; and with their examples, Drew Hayden Taylor approaches the question of representational agency from both sides of an ethnic line. As a result, while the issue of voice is central to the question of representation (which would grant the Warrior the right to speak for the Native community, while it would be denied to Summer), Linda Alcoff's general warning against "speaking for others" is reaffirmed: even a Native person cannot simply represent a large ethnic group. Furthermore, Taylor adds another representational twist to the Warrior by statements such as "I live where the sun shines. Where the rain falls. Where the wind blows. I am there" (*B* 59). If, as Robert Nunn has done for this play's prequel *(The Baby Blues)* the role of Summer is identified as implicitly mocking "the romantic notions of the 'authentic Indian'" ("Hybridity" 109), and if "to play such statements back is an act of mimicry that questions their authority" ("Hybridity" 109), the Warrior in *The Buz'Gem Blues* even presents a double form of postcolonial mimicry by "playing back" such colonial statements from the stance of Native-authorized traditionalism. Through this double twist, the Warrior holds up a mirror to all intercultural criticism, becoming a cleverly arranged site that questions postethnicity and authentication in general: If a Cree person precariously chooses to impersonate exactly the same stereotypical representations of Nativeness that had pervaded the European-American imagination and its market for centuries, where are the limits to performances of Native identity?

6. *Trans-Differently Playing With "Academia Mania": Drew Hayden Taylor's Trickster Performances*

Although Drew Hayden Taylor has repeatedly made fun of non-Native academics' inclination toward finding trickster figures and metaphors in Native texts – a practice termed the "Spot-the-Trickster Syndrome" by Daniel David Moses (see Taylor, "Canoeing" 28 and "Native Themes" 7) –

and although he has explicitly "tried to avoid trickster imagery completely, just because again, I think it's another over-used cliché" (Däwes 12), there is no denying that trickster discourse strongly permeates his texts.

Within the inner system of communication, to use Manfred Pfister's classic distinction (see Pfister 50f; 152), Taylor's characters explore the performative dimensions and limits of Hollingerian "postethnic" identities by negotiating their chosen affiliations with others. Like laboratories of intra- and transcultural exchange, *Toronto at Dreamer's Rock, alterNatives,* and *The Buz'Gem Blues* manifest the relevance and necessity of dialogue in the trying and testing of authenticity and the subsequent questioning of given power systems. In their variety of approaches to the dynamics of authenticity, these plays wittily uncover the identity labels of everyday life not as existential fixities but merely as masks with a market value, more often than not instrumentalized for personal needs. Acting out the strong force of humour as a perfect strategy to expose the relativity of all positions, as well as to subvert the discursive processes of domination, most of Drew Hayden Taylor's figures experience that to identify and speak for oneself is a basic human right which should not be sold out for labels of political correctness. Beyond the stage and in the outer system of communication, however, these plays achieve much more than their concomitant appeal for universal inter-human respect.

If Angel's and Professor Savage's powers extend beyond their stories to include the plays that frame them, they certainly also reach out beyond the form of the play itself. Whether this communal interaction happens more or less overtly, all three plays extend their range of deconstruction across theatrical borderlines and invite the audience to join their project of questioning the hierarchies behind cultural identity, to unravel their mechanisms of power, and to break the silences of the unspeakable. On another level, therefore, the irony acted out by the characters provokes a critical awareness of authenticity's (or "reality's") discursive foundation and provides an incentive not to take its ideologies too seriously. Additionally, through the deconstructive, self-ironic openness that is so perfectly symbolized by the trickster sign, the plays eventually direct their viewfinders against themselves as further instances of representation: as all forms of identity negotiation, these, too, are unstable semiotic sites of play. And, unsurprisingly, we find Drew Hayden Taylor on the other side of the signifying chain, continuously contributing to a "theatre of representation" in its double sense. Mocking the ideologies of authenticity, he is known to manifest his authority as "Drew Hayden Taylor – Aboriginal Attitude and

Attributes Assessor (DHT: AAAA)" ("How Native" 105), to label himself a "NAIFNI: Native / Aboriginal / Indigenous / First Nations / Indian" ("First Annual" 44) or even to invent his own community:

> This is a declaration of independence, my declaration of independence. I've spent too many years explaining who and what I am repeatedly, so as of this moment, I officially secede from both races. I plan to start my own separate nation. Because I am half Ojibway, and half Caucasian, we will be called the Occasions. And I, of course, since I'm founding the new nation, will be a Special Occasion. "Pretty" 439

Through these ultimately self-referential stagings, Drew Hayden Taylor's performances expose the absences inherent in all representations and simulations, doing justice to the theoretical achievements of postcolonial criticism by understanding identity as a simultaneously communicational, psychological, economic, and political act of signification, yet with all the poststructuralist and political implications that this equation bears. As such, Drew Hayden Taylor's performative project is part of what Gerald Vizenor calls "the stories of native endurance and survivance; the stories that create a sense of presence, a native self, a teasable self in names, relations, and native contingencies, but not victimry. That sense of self is a creation, an aesthetic presence; the self is not an essence, or immanence, but the mien of stories" (*Fugitive*

Poses 20). Most significantly, in its ironic, self-reflexive use of variant poses, the performance of Taylor's theatrical figures (including himself as *auteur*) is *différant*, pointing back at itself and beyond to lay open its signifying character, and as such it turns into a project which – like Breinig's and Lösch's stance of *transdifference* – allows for the simultaneity of conflicting positions, undermines dichotomies and clearly warns against the hierarchical implications of all certainties: the strategic project of the trickster.

Notes

1 This article contains ideas from a former approach of mine which was previously published as "Local or Global? Negotiations of Identity in Drew Hayden Taylor's Plays," *Global Challenges and Regional Responses in Contemporary Drama in English,* ed. Jochen Achilles, Ina Bergmann, and Birgit Däwes (Trier: WVT, 2003) 217-31. I would like to express my particular appreciation to Robert Nunn and Drew Hayden Taylor for their feedback as well as their inspiring questions and comments. As Rusty in *Toronto at Dreamer's Rock* would put it: "Meegwetch."

2 This contrast to (the equally present) Native theatre in the U.S.A. is also illustrated by the fact that while the *Oxford Companion to American Literature* in 1995 does not feature one single entry on indigenous drama, the *Oxford Companion to Canadian Literature* only two years later offers an abundance of entries on indigenous writers and movements.

3   Besides, as Dominique Legros points out, most contemporary Native cultures are marked "inauthentic" because of their temporal distance to pre-colonization traditions, which not only assigns them a clearly inferior place in the hierarchy of cultures but simply undercuts the cultural authority of any indigenous people (see Legros 131).

4   Don B. Wilmeth identifies "almost 600 plays, many lost, from 1606 to the present" which include Native characters or themes (128).

5   In my use of the term "indigenism" I am following Arnold Krupat who identifies it as one of the three dominant contemporary perspectives on Native culture. Its key element is "a particular relation to the earth as underlying a worldview that can be called traditional or tribal" (91).

6   In light of Bobby's subversiveness it is probably no coincidence that it was his favourite philosopher, Friedrich Nietzsche, who stated in 1870 that the subject – as all human truths – is a fiction; a necessary illusion to keep us psychologically functioning, but an illusion all the same (see Nietzsche 881).

7   "Buz'Gem" is the Ojibway word denoting "boyfriend" or "girlfriend."

8   Vizenor's terminology particularly points to the simulative and performative character of all representation: "The indian is a simulation; the absence of natives, the indian transposes the real, and the simulation of the real has no referent, memories or native stories" (*Fugitive Poses* 15).

WORKS CITED

Alcoff, Linda. "The Problem of Speaking for Others." *Cultural Critique* 20 (Winter 1991/92): 5-32.

Breinig, Helmbrecht. "Introduction: Culture, Economy, and Identity Locations – Representations of Difference and Transdifference." *Imaginary (Re-)Locations: Tradition, Moder-*

nity, and the Market in Contemporary Native American Literature and Culture. Ed. Helmbrecht Breinig. Tübingen: Stauffenburg, 2003. 19-46.

—— and Klaus Lösch. "Introduction: Difference and Transdifference." *Multiculturalism in Contemporary Societies: Perspectives on Difference and Transdifference.* Ed. Helmbrecht Breinig, Jürgen Gebhardt, and Klaus Lösch. Erlangen: Universitätsbibliothek, 2002. 11-36.

Bush, George W. "State of the Union Address." *The White House Press Releases.* January 29, 2002. April 20, 2004. <http://www.whitehouse.gov/news/releases/2002/01/20020129-11.html>.

Chomsky, Noam. "Reflections on 9-11." *9-11.* New York: Open Media, 2002. 119-28.

Churchill, Ward. *Fantasies of the Master Race: Literature, Cinema, and the Colonization of American Indians.* Monroe, ME: Common Courage Press, 1992.

Däwes, Birgit. "An Interview with Drew Hayden Taylor." *Contemporary Literature* 44.1 (Spring 2003): 1-18.

Flynn, Joyce. "Academics on the Trail of The Stage 'Indian': A Review Essay." *Studies in American Indian Literatures* 11.1 (Winter 1987): 1-16.

Glaap, Albert Reiner. "Drew Hayden Taylor's Dramatic Career." *Siting the Other: Re-Visions of Marginality in Australian and English-Canadian Drama.* Ed. Marc Maufort and Franca Bellarsi. Brussels: Peter Lang, 2001. 217-32.

——. "Margo Kane, Daniel David Moses, Yvette Nolan, Drew Hayden Taylor: Four Native Playwrights from Canada." *Anglistik: Mitteilungen des Verbandes deutscher Anglisten* 7.1 (March 1996): 5-25.

Glancy, Diane. "Further (Farther): Creating a Dialogue to Talk About Native American Plays." *Journal of Dramatic Theory and Criticism* 14.1 (1999): 143-49.

Grice, H. Paul. "Logic and Conversation." *Speech Acts. Vol. 3: Syntax and Semantics.* Ed. Peter Cole and Jerry L. Morgan. New York: Academic Press, 1975. 41-58.

Hollinger, David. *Postethnic America: Beyond Multiculturalism*. New York: Basic Books, 1995.

Krupat, Arnold. "Nationalism, Indigenism, Cosmopolitanism: Three Critical Perspectives on Native American Literatures." *Imaginary (Re-)Locations: Tradition, Modernity, and the Market in Contemporary Native American Literature and Culture*. Ed. Helmbrecht Breinig. Tübingen: Stauffenburg, 2003. 87-106.

Legros, Dominique. "First Nation Postmodern Cultures: (Re)Constructing the (De)Con-structed and Celebrating the Changes." *Mirror Writing: (Re-)Constructions of Native American Identity*. Ed. Thomas Claviez and Maria Moss. Berlin: Galda + Wilch, 2000. 125-54.

Lösch, Klaus. "Cultural Identity, Territory, and the Discursive Location of Native American Fiction." *Imaginary (Re-)Locations: Tradition, Modernity, and the Market in Contemporary Native American Literature and Culture*. Ed. Helmbrecht Breinig. Tübingen: Stauffenburg, 2003. 63-80.

Lutz, Hartmut. "Native American Studies in Europe: Caught Between 'Indianthusiasm' and Scholarship." *ZENAF Arbeits- und Forschungsbericht* 1 (December 2000): 13-25.

Nietzsche, Friedrich. "Über Wahrheit und Lüge im außermoralischen Sinne." *Werke: Die Geburt der Tragödie; Unzeitgemäße Betrachtungen I-IV; Nachgelassene Schriften 1870-73*. Ed. Giorgio Colli and Mazzino Montinari. München: dtv, 1988. 875-90.

Nunn, Robert. "Drew Hayden Taylor's alterNatives: Dishing the Dirt." *Crucible of Cultures: Anglophone Drama at the Dawn of a New Millennium*. Ed. Marc Maufort and Franca Bellarsi. Dramaturgies 4. Brussels: Peter Lang, 2002. 209-17.

—. "Hybridity and Mimicry in the Plays of Drew Hayden Taylor." *Essays on Canadian Writing* 65 (Fall 1998): 95-119.

Pfister, Manfred. *Das Drama*. 1977. 10th ed. München: Fink, 2000.

Rathbun, Paul Roland. "American Indian Dramaturgy: Situating Native Presence on the American Stage." Ph.D. diss. University of Wisconsin, Madison, 1996.

Schlesinger, Arthur, Jr. *The Disuniting of America: Reflections on a Multicultural Society*. 1991. Rev. ed. New York: Norton, 1998.

Shanley, Kathryn W. "The Indians America Loves to Love and Read: American Indian Identity and Cultural Appropriation." *American Indian Quarterly* 21.4 (Fall 1997): 675-702.

Spivak, Gayatri Chakravorty. *Outside in the Teaching Machine*. New York: Routledge, 1993.

Taylor, Charles. "The Politics of Recognition." *Multiculturalism: Examining the Politics of Recognition*. Ed. Amy Gutmann. Princeton: Princeton University Press, 1994. 25-73.

Taylor, Drew Hayden. "Academia Mania." *Funny, You Don't Look Like One: Observations from a Blue-Eyed Ojibway*. Rev. ed. Penticton, BC: Theytus Books, 1998. 95-99.

——. "Alive and Well: Native Theatre in Canada." *American Indian Theater in Performance: A Reader*. Ed. Hanay Geiogamah and Jaye T. Darby. Los Angeles: UCLA American Indian Studies Center, 2000. 256-64.

——. *alterNatives*. Burnaby, BC: Talonbooks, 2000. [Parenthetically cited as A]

——. *The Buz'Gem Blues*. Vancouver: Talonbooks, 2002. [Parenthetically cited as B]

——. "Canoeing the Rivers of Canadian Aboriginal Theatre: The Portages and Pitfalls." *Crucible of Cultures: Anglophone Drama at the Dawn of a New Millennium*. Ed. Marc Maufort and Franca Bellarsi. Brussels: Peter Lang, 2002. 25-29.

——. "The First Annual Aboriginal Trivia Contest." *Further Adventures of a Blue-Eyed Ojibway: Funny, You Don't Look Like One Two*. Penticton, BC: Theytus Books, 1999. 44-46.

——. "How Native is Native if you're Native?" *Further Adventures of a Blue-Eyed Ojibway: Funny, You Don't Look Like One Two*. Penticton, BC: Theytus Books, 1999. 104-07.

———. "Native Themes 101." *CanPlay* 19.2 (March–April 2002): 6-7.

———. "Pretty Like a White Boy: The Adventures of a Blue Eyed Ojibway." *An Anthology of Canadian Native Literature in English*. 2nd ed. Ed. Daniel David Moses and Terry Goldie. Toronto: Oxford University Press, 1998. 436-39.

———. "Storytelling to Stage: The Growth of Native Theatre in Canada." *The Drama Review* 41.3 (Fall 1997): 140-52.

———. *Toronto at Dreamer's Rock and Education Is Our Right: Two One-Act Plays*. Saskatoon, Saskatchewan: Fifth House Publishers, 1990. Also published in Germany: *Toronto at Dreamer's Rock*. Ed. Albert Reiner Glaap. Literarische Texte für den Englischunterricht der Sekundarstufe II. Berlin: Cornelsen, 1995. [Parenthetical references (T) are to the former edition].

Theobald, Elizabeth. "Their Desperate Need for Noble Savages." *The Drama Review* 41.3 (Fall 1997): 142-43.

Vizenor, Gerald. *Fugitive Poses: Native American Indian Scenes of Absence and Presence*. Lincoln: University of Nebraska Press, 1998.

———. *Manifest Manners: Postindian Warriors of Survivance*. Hanover, NH: Wesleyan University Press, 1994.

———. "Ruins of Representation: Shadow Survivance and the Literature of Dominance." *American Indian Quarterly* 17.1 (Winter 1993): 7-30.

Wilmeth, Don B. "Noble or Ruthless Savage? The American Indian on Stage and in the Drama." *American Indian Theater in Performance: A Reader*. Ed. Hanay Geiogamah and Jaye T. Darby. Los Angeles: UCLA American Indian Studies Center, 2000. 127-56.

Drew Hayden Taylor's *alterNatives*

Dishing the Dirt

ROBERT NUNN

> While writing this play, I was fully expecting to become the Salman Rushdie of the Native community, for I'm sure there is something in this play to annoy everybody. Part of my goal was to create unsympathetic characters right across the board. And to do this, as the saying goes, I had to break some eggs. A close friend, a Native woman, came up to me quite angry and said, "So this is what you really think of Native people!" Then some time later, one reviewer referred to it as "witless white bashing." Evidently I have become a racist! Further proof that you never know how your day is gonna end (Taylor, "Foreword" 6).

Drew Hayden Taylor's plays have always gotten at serious themes through gently subversive humour. One recent play, *alterNatives,* however, is not nearly as gentle.[1] The tricksterish characteristics of Taylor's dramaturgy, about which I wrote in a previous essay,[2] remain present, but the emphasis lies not so much on playful inversion as on turning the world upside down in order to do it real damage.[3] By the play's end, the dinner party, which the audience watches from start to finish, has very possibly left a friendship, a relationship, and a marriage in ruins. The foremost but not the only agent of this mayhem is the appropriately named Bobby

Rabbit, self-styled "Uber-Indian" and "alterNative Warrior." In this essay, I would like to explore the play through the lens of Lewis Hyde's *Trickster Makes This World: Mischief, Myth, and Art,* in particular through the notion that Trickster throws dirt around – the dirt that a social order rejects in order to protect its purified idea of itself. Neither whites nor Natives are spared the pain of having their dirt thrown in their faces. In brief, Lewis Hyde's argument runs as follows:

> [W]e begin to wonder if there is any way to make a general rule about what is dirt and what is not. The anthropologist Mary Douglas ... suggests we go back to an old saying: "Dirt is matter out of place." ... To this first definition of dirt, Douglas adds a second: dirt is the anomalous, not just what is out of place but what has no place at all when we are done making sense of our world ... In either of Douglas's cases – out of place or anomalous – the point to underline here is that dirt is always a by-product of creating order. Where there is dirt, there is always a system of some kind, and rules about dirt are meant to preserve it ... whenever humans or gods move ... to protect order completely from the dirt that is its by-product, trickster will upset their plans. (175-79)

The other aspect of "dirt-work" that Hyde addresses is "shameless speech." Matter out of place is kept in its place by codes of silence hedged about by shame. Trickster breaks these taboos by speaking without shame about the dirt that nobody is supposed to talk about, let alone notice. Hyde writes:

You and I know when to speak and when to hold the tongue, but Old Man Coyote doesn't. He has no tact. They're all the same, these tricksters; they have no shame and so they have no silence. (153)

In *alterNatives,* Bobby Rabbit embodies that shameless speaker *par excellence.* Here follows a typical example of Bobby at work. He recounts his conversation with a priest and two nuns on a bus:

So we started talking religious stuff, you know, all nicey nicey. And then I calmly asked them about their personal perspective on the difference between original sin and ab-original sin. Ab-original sin meaning that being born Native was a horrible affront to God and the Church, paganism and all that. And it had to be corrected as harshly as possible. I went into the whole Jesuit invasion, the Residential school system. You know, the usual . . . Surprisingly, they weren't as receptive as I had hoped. (61-62)

Bobby *will not shut up* about anything where he senses the presence of a conspiracy of silence to avoid all mention of "matter out of place." This is what he calls being an "Uber-Indian," or "alterNative Warrior," a concept he has cobbled together out of Nietzsche, Native tradition, and "a natural flair for turning institutions and people on their ear" (54). The dinner party at the centre of *alterNatives* requires a lot of tact in order not to fly apart, as a brief description of the dramatis personae will indicate. Colleen, a professor of Native Literature, has been living with Angel, an aspiring Native writer, for some months. She is Jewish, Angel is Ojibway. In the play, they are throwing their first dinner party. Colleen has invited her old friend Michelle and her husband Dale, both non-Native. Michelle tends to get really drunk really fast, especially when there is tension in the air. Dale is a well-meaning blunderer. Colleen has also invited surprise guests, two friends of Angel's, whom she has never met: Yvonne and Bobby, both Native. Neither of them has seen Angel since he abruptly left them shortly before he met Colleen. Yvonne and Angel are former lovers. Bobby once considered Angel a fellow Warrior. Angel's disappearance still rankles with both of them. It would take a miracle to make this party go smoothly. Bobby's presence guarantees that the evening will be disastrous.

The relentless "dirt-work" that dooms this party has many targets, but Bobby leads the attack on one in particular, namely the notion of "Authentic Aboriginality." As Alan Filewod points out, the term "Aboriginality" only exists in the context of colonialism. No people are called – or call themselves – Aboriginal, unless colonized: "the very notion of aboriginality . . . is itself a category of understanding introduced by colonialism" (365). Bobby relentlessly treats aboriginality as an effect of colonialism, as we saw in his query about ab-original sin. He is scarcely in the door before he asks, "So who do I have to sign a treaty with to get a drink around here?" (44). Whether aboriginality is a term applied by the colonists, or adopted by the colonized themselves, it remains fraught with complexities and contradictions, which are routinely swept under the rug. The most basic simplification consists in lumping many nations which differ profoundly from each other under a single heading, such as "Indian." In *alterNatives,* white assumptions of a single homogeneous Native identity come under attack, and from a variety of directions. Taylor's targets range from straightforwardly stupid questions to less obvious assumptions, such as Native opinions on non-Native appropriations of Native voice. In the following excerpt, Dale, speaking to Angel, offers a good example of the stupid question: "We used to know a Native person, didn't we Michelle? . . . Benita. It was Benita. That's it. Benita . . . something. I don't suppose you know a Benita?" (27). A more covert form of simplification is exposed in the following passage:

> YVONNE: Dare I mention W. P. Kinsella?[4]
> COLLEEN: We won't even get into that. I'm a hundred percent on your side about him.
> YVONNE: My side? How do you even know what side I'm on?
> COLLEEN: Well . . . uh . . . I assumed because of the controversy surrounding his work . . . And you're First Nations . . . (51)

And running through the play is the question of how to cook moose. Colleen, who has bought a moose roast for the dinner, assumes that Angel, as a "Native Aboriginal First Nations Indigenous person" (17), will know how to cook it. But she turns out to be badly wrong: Angel's contribution to the dinner is to bake the Jewish delicacy rugelach, whilst the expert on moose happens to be Dale.

Everywhere in the play, there are moments when the gross oversimplification implicit in the concept of "aboriginality" gets dismantled, allowing suppressed differences to come out of hiding. Although she does not appear as abrasive as Bobby, Yvonne is a "dirt-worker" too, but whereas Bobby's targets are white, Yvonne's are Native as well as white. She describes her M.A. thesis topic to Colleen: "The working title is 'Selective Traditionalism and the Emergence of the Narrow-Focused Cultural Revival.'" She goes on to explain:

> In the last thirty years or so, there has been an amazing cultural revival happening. Languages, practices and traditions, once banned, are not [sic] being embraced with almost a fanatical enthusiasm. This in itself is good. Great in fact. We support that . . . [But] Look a little closer at that picture. In their hurry to recapture the old days of our Grandfathers and grandmothers, these people are being very selective about which traditions they choose to follow, often excluding many ancient practices that would not be considered politically correct in today's society . . . Centuries ago there were ar-ranged marriages,

> frequent intertribal warfare, slavery, and in some cases, rumours of cannibalism. These are not even mentioned at Pow wows or Elder's conferences. It's as if they didn't exist. It's become a form of cultural hypocrisy . . . [B]ecause I explore these areas, some people think I'm sabotaging the traditions, or being disrespectful. I am as proud of who I am and where I come from as the next Nish. But I can't believe it's so wrong to ask these simple questions. (75-78)

Yvonne points out that the Peterborough Petroglyphs, which were "carved somewhere between five hundred and a thousand years ago" (77), are under the custodial care of the Curve Lake First Nation, in other words of Ojibways who migrated to Central Ontario in the 1820s and who have no connection whatever with the people who created the carvings. The subtext of this arrangement, from Yvonne's perspective, does not seem so far removed from "We used to know a Native person, her name was Benita, do you know her?"[5]

The other term subjected to scrutiny in this play is "authenticity," equally an effect of colonialism. It too is forced to disgorge a lot of dirt. Criteria of authenticity have been regularly imposed by the settler culture on Natives: in a kind of sleight of hand which hides the reality of colonial aggression, "authentic" Native culture is taken to amount to only that which remains uncontaminated by contact with the settler culture. As Terry Goldie explains, it is whites, not Indigenes, who test indigenous culture for authenticity: "A corollary of the temporal split between this golden age [pre-contact indigenous culture] and the present degradation is to see indigenous culture as true, pure, and static. Whatever fails this test is not really a part of that culture" (17). On the other side of the fence, an "authentically" Native cultural identity can be constructed by First Nations people as an act of "strategic essentialism" – Gayatri Spivak's term – countering the identity imposed by colonialist discourse with a discursive construct of one's own (Ashcroft et al. 79). The intractable problem for both cultures is the actual hybrid nature of contemporary Native cultures. White criteria of authenticity discount signs of hybridity as "degradation" or "corruption": as Alan Filewod argues, "mediation (most commonly by urbanization and postcolonial deracination)" is often seen by white critics of contemporary Native art as "the condition that diminishes the authenticity of a culture. In this essentialist and humanist view (which owes much to Rousseau), the more authentic the culture, the less mediated it is" (364-65). Meanwhile, Native construction of strategic essentialism can equally fall into the same trap of dismissing hybridity. For as Gareth Griffiths points out, "markers of cultural difference may well be perceived as authentic cultural signifiers, but that claim to authenticity can imply that these cultures are not subject to change" (Ashcroft et al. 21). Angel, for instance, is attacked from both sides for wanting to write science fiction. He has abandoned Bobby and Yvonne partly because Bobby kept "urging me ... no, practically ordering me to quit wasting my time on my silly stories and write something that would help the 'cause'" (103-104). He has left them to live with Colleen, who insists "You have such potential, you could create the great Canadian aboriginal novel, but instead you want to squander it away on this silly genre" (102). Somehow there is no room within "authentic" aboriginal identity for such a hybrid as a Native science-fiction writer. The problem with Angel's desire to write science fiction throws the problem with essentialism, strategic or otherwise, into high relief. As does the problem of how to cook moose. That piece of meat shows how an inanimate object can be an effective dirt-worker. At the very beginning of the play, its presence on the menu brings the issue of white criteria of Native authenticity into the open:

> COLLEEN: I really wish you had helped me prepare the moose.
> ANGEL: I don't do moose ...
> COLLEEN: ... I put the moose in at three-hundred-and-fifty degrees. Does that sound okay?
> ANGEL: I told you, I don't know.
> COLLEEN: What kind of Native Aboriginal First Nations Indigenous person are you?

ANGEL: One of that large tribe that's never had a need, a reason or an opportunity to cook a moose roast in its life. In my case, that's what mothers were for.
COLLEEN: Too bad. I just thought it would have been more authentic.
ANGEL: The roast or me? (16-17)

But the worst beating "authenticity" takes in this play is not revealed until the end. Angel's mysterious unwillingness to tell Colleen what reserve he is from becomes finally cleared up when Angel takes a book from Colleen's shelf and tells how it came to be written. It is a collection of Ojibway legends, harvested at the Curve Lake reserve when he was a boy. In fact, he belonged to a group of several boys on the reserve who were approached by white researchers and asked to recount ancient legends, since the elders of the community refused to tell them any. For fifty cents a legend, they complied:

ANGEL: We told some great legends, huh? Fantastic stories that only an eleven-year-old could come up with. And that's what we did. We made them up. We would take the fifty cents they gave us, go to the store and buy pop, chips, popsicles, all sorts of garbage, sit around on the church steps, and make up the story we'd tell them the next day. (129)

The first time Angel picked up the book, he was shocked to find at least four of these made-up stories, and to discover that the book is in its seventh printing, that it actually features on the reading list of a half dozen university Native Literature courses, and that Native teachers are teaching the book to Native students. Colleen teaches it too. Bobby was the ringleader, whilst Colleen, then a young graduate student, belonged to the research team. Angel remembers her buying him an ice-cream cone. She has not, until this moment, recognized him. So the search by white researchers for authentic – that is, uncontaminated – Native culture has harvested a pack of lies told by eleven-year-old boys out of sheer mischief. Colleen is devastated. Angel feels guilty. He reproaches Bobby for instigating this, accusing him of spending his whole life playing "stupid little games ... to make fun of people" (130). So much for the "alterNative Warrior."

Just a minute though. Is this not just the sort of thing that Trickster is constantly doing? The fallout from this trick calls into question all the unspoken assumptions – and exclusions – underlying the very concept "authentic," just the kind of dirt-work Trickster loves to perform. And it would not be the first time that Trickster has passed off wildly inventive lies as the real article, as a reading of Paul Radin's study of the Winnebago trickster cycle makes abundantly clear. Maybe this mischief is as "authentic" an expression of Ojibway culture as the old legends, with this difference: the legends belong to the past – otherwise they do not count

– while the boys' inventions are of the living and changing – and hybrid – culture of the present.

Angel may reject Bobby and all his destructive games, but I would argue that the play does not. Bobby is the character who keeps everything on edge, challenges every given, turns simplistic categories inside out, and creates a really impressive chaos out of a nice dinner party. In his study of the trickster in Shakespeare, Richard Hillman suggests that while Trickster's mayhem may lead to a revitalized order, no such higher purpose should be attributed to Trickster himself. His destructiveness only has the potential to renew life, but is not engaged in with that aim:

> [T]he trickster's creativity is indeed part of his significance, but he is essentially "undifferentiated," and in many of his particular adventures he is merely destructive. This is where the subversive principle, as I conceive it, conflicts with the reassuring teleological orientation of more traditional "festive" criticism, such as C.L. Barber's, according to which "ritual" disorder already contains its own undoing. My view presupposes that whether the potential is realized . . . is contingent precisely on his spontaneous and unconditional embracing of what appears to be merely destructive. In order for there to be power, there must be danger, not merely some form of circumscribed and more-or-less tolerated misrule. (14)

Bobby has certainly left a trail of destruction behind him. Whether the relationship between

Angel and Colleen will weather this storm is doubtful. Colleen's sense that Angel incarnates "The Authentic Indian" (with a little help from her) has been seriously shaken. Angel has countered her assumptions with a demonstration that Colleen, in spite of being Jewish, knows far more about Native culture and language than about her own cultural roots. The questions: "Are you with me because I'm Native?" and "Are you with me because I'm white?" (135) receive no answer, and how could they, when this evening has forced each of them to recognize what a hybrid the other really is. It seems equally uncertain whether Michelle and Dale's marriage will survive the revelation that Dale has had enough of being Michelle's prize convert to the cause of vegetarianism – that roast of moose at work again. It is even less certain that Angel will renew his membership in the "alterNative Warriors." But, interestingly enough, the play ends on an almost upbeat note. Angel, the only member of the dinner party left in the apartment, is joined by Dale, and the two of them – the Native carnivorous science-fiction writer and the non-Native vegetarian science-fiction fan – sit down to a plate of perfectly cooked moose. There is a mood of peace and sensual enjoyment, in which Angel tells a story that sounds like an unashamed hybrid of Native concerns and science-fiction conventions. Two men who may have just lost a great deal are content to savour the moment calmly, and face perhaps a very different future. "alterNative" humour may have been destructive, but not merely so. This play constitutes a sort of rite of passage. Characters who lived a life overly free of dirt have had it thrown in their faces: as the saying goes, their certainties have been destroyed, but truth, which embraces anomalies, contradictions, and "matter out of place," proves greater than certainty, and much more alive. And I sustain the thesis that the "matter out of place" in this play is colonialism's byproduct.

I would like to conclude with some speculation about the relation between "alterNative" humour and postcolonial resistance. Drew Hayden Taylor's comedies are not isolated instances of Native humour, while everybody else is writing ultra-serious books with titles like *Bury My Heart at Wounded Knee*, *The Dispossessed* or *How a People Die* (Angel by the way has hidden the latter in the freezer). Taylor forms a part of a wave of new visibility of Native humour (I mean of course new to non-Natives): Tomson Highway's plays and novel, and Thomas King's fiction and his five-year run of the radio program *The Dead Dog Café Comedy Hour*, represent two other major examples. Taylor recently produced a film on Native humour for the National Film Board of Canada, titled *Redskins, Tricksters and Puppy Stew*. Allan J. Ryan borrows the term "the trickster shift" from Carl Beam to title his study of humour and irony in contemporary Native art. These works and many others celebrate Trickster humour as a revived element of Native culture: "Weesageechak begins to dance," as the Toronto theatre company Native Earth Performing Arts titles its annual festival of new work. Indeed, Tomson Highway claims that "Without the continued presence of this extraordinary figure [the Trickster], the core of Indian culture would be gone forever" (12-13). I would argue that the Trickster seems particularly apt at negotiating the perilous relation between Aboriginal cultures and their post-colonial situation. He does so by subverting the colonizer's essentializing gaze, by preventing the strategic essentialism of the colonized from hardening into a rigid ahistorical identity, and by revelling in the impurity and hybridity that the colonizer habitually dismisses as "degradation." By its very nature, colonialism is an order that has had to pretend that mountains of dirt do not exist, through such means as the Freudian dream-mechanism of "distortion," about which Homi K. Bhabha writes in his celebrated essay "Signs Taken for Wonders." As "dirt-worker" *extraordinaire* and "alterNative warrior," the postcolonial Trickster has his work cut out for him: to put the non-Native spectator (such as myself obviously) on the couch, so to speak, and oblige him or her to work backward through distortion to the latent content of colonialism; and at the same time, to affirm a living, changing Native culture. Trickster humour cuts both ways.

NOTES

1 An earlier version of this essay was published in *Crucible of Cultures: Anglophone Drama at the Dawn of a New Millennium,* ed. Marc Maufort and Franca Bellarsi (Brussels: P. I. E. Peter Lang, 2002) 209-218.
2 Robert Nunn, "Hybridity and Mimicry in the Plays of Drew Hayden Taylor," *Essays in Canadian Writing* 65 (Fall 1998): 95-119.
3 *alterNatives* (1999) does not signify a shift in Taylor's dramaturgy so much as a broadening of scope. More recent plays indeed cover a wide range. *The Buz'Gem Blues* (2001) returns to several of the characters of *The Baby Blues* (1995) in the same vein of gentle satire, while *Toronto@Dreamer'sRock.com* (1999) offers a very dark sequel to the optimistic *Toronto at Dreamer's Rock* of 1989. *Sucker Falls* (2001) is an adaptation of Brecht and Weill's *The Rise and Fall of the City of Mahagonny*. The dates given are those of the first performance.
4 W. P. Kinsella is a non-Native Canadian author, best known for his novel *Shoeless Joe* (1982). He has published several collections of humourous stories set in the fictional Ermineskin First Nation in Hobbema, Alberta, including *Dance Me Outside* (1977) and *The Fencepost Chronicles* (1986).
5 On the white side of the ledger, Yvonne does a piece of dirt-work on *Star Trek,* comparing the space ship Enterprise's constantly violated "Prime Directive" of non-interference with indigenous cultures to the Spanish colonialists' "Requiermento," the document read in

Spanish to indigenous peoples in the Americas prior to attacking them. Both documents, she argues, exist to exculpate the invaders (106-108).

WORKS CITED

Ashcroft, Bill, Gareth Griffiths and Helen Tiffin. *Key Concepts in Post-Colonial Studies.* London: Routledge, 1998.

Bhabha, Homi K. "Signs Taken for Wonders: Questions of Ambivalence and Authority under a Tree outside Delhi, May 1817." *Europe and its Others. Proc. of the Essex Conference on the Sociology of Literature, July 1984.* Ed. Francis Barker et al. Colchester: U of Essex, 1985. 89-106.

Filewod, Alan. "Receiving Aboriginality: Tomson Highway and the Crisis of Cultural Authority." *Theatre Journal* 46 (1994): 363-73.

Goldie, Terry. *Fear and Temptation: The Image of the Indigene in Canadian, Australian, and New Zealand Literatures.* Kingston: McGill-Queen's University Press, 1989.

Highway, Tomson. *Dry Lips Oughta Move to Kapuskasing.* Saskatoon: Fifth House, 1989.

Hillman, Richard. *Shakespearean Subversions: The Trickster and the Play-Text.* London: Routledge, 1992.

Hyde, Lewis. *Trickster Makes This World: Mischief, Myth, and Art.* New York: Farrar, Straus and Giroux, 1998.

Nunn, Robert. "Hybridity and Mimicry in the Plays of Drew Hayden Taylor." *Essays in Canadian Writing* 65 (Fall 1998): 95-119.

Radin, Paul. *The Trickster: A Study in American Indian Mythology.* London: Routledge, 1956.

Ryan, Allan J. *The Trickster Shift: Humour and Irony in Contemporary Native Art.* Vancouver: University of British Columbia Press, 1999.

Spivak, Gayatri. "Criticism, Feminism and the Institution." Interview with Elizabeth Gross. *Thesis Eleven* 10/11 (November-March 1984-85): 175-87. Cited in *Key Con-*

cepts in Post-Colonial Studies by Bill Ashcroft, Gareth Griffiths, and Helen Tiffin. London: Routledge, 1998. 79.

Taylor, Drew Hayden. *alterNatives.* Vancouver: Talonbooks, 2000.

From Copper Woman to Grey Owl to the alterNative Warrior

Exploring Voice and the Need to Connect

JONATHAN R. DEWAR

It can be argued that Drew Hayden Taylor's play *alterNatives* covers too much ground; many issues are glossed over, although this is in keeping with the superficiality of the dinner conversation. It is also controversial, as Taylor himself points out in his introduction, with something to annoy everybody. Nevertheless, *alterNatives* is a worthy text to teach in a Native literature or a Canadian literature course. It should fit in nicely with the curricula already being taught ad infinitum in English departments, including works such as George Ryga's *The Ecstasy of Rita Joe,* W.P. Kinsella's *Dance Me Outside,* and Duncan Campbell Scott's "Indian poems." I would never argue for the rejection of any of these texts (except in a course on Native literature – that is, literature by Native writers) but would insist on teaching them within the proper context, including the role these texts have played in confusing the notion of Native voice in literature. Proceeding from a discussion of Taylor's *alter-*

Natives and the central issues that the text raises, I will move to a discussion of a troublesome text I encountered a few years ago in a course on Commonwealth women writers, Anne Cameron's *Daughters of Copper Woman,* and a text I brought to the classroom, Armand Garnet Ruffo's *Grey Owl: The Mystery of Archie Belaney.* As a person of mixed heritage, I have often turned to texts that deal thematically with issues of (re)connection to culture to help me articulate my position within the discourse and navigate my way through the many intersecting debates. Both of these texts, Cameron's and Ruffo's, are two such books, although they may initially seem worlds apart. Cameron, a White woman, immerses herself in a Native narrator/alter ego, and Ruffo, an Anishnaabe writer, presents a fictionalized and stylized biography of Canada's famous Indian impostor, Grey Owl, problematizing both the notion of voice and connection.

In Hayden Taylor's *alterNatives,* six characters engage in a lively, spirited, no-holds-barred "debate" that covers more ground than your average short play, but not nearly the amount of ground covered by your average treaty. This "punny," "jokey" opening is liable to be read in a few different ways, perhaps as offensive, perhaps not. And it is this writer's amateurish attempt to convey the spirit of Taylor's tone: *alterNatives* is funny, but it is also challenging, deeply personal (although Taylor provides a similarly humorous caveat in his introduction: "Any resemblance to people, dead or alive, is purely coincidental. Honest Injun!" (6)), and, by his own admission, "unsympathetic." He says,

> While writing this play, I was fully expecting to become the Salman Rushdie of the Native community, for I'm sure there is something in this play to annoy everybody. Part of my goal was to create unsympathetic characters right across the board. And to do this, as the saying goes, I had to break a few eggs. A close friend, a Native woman, came up to me quite angry and said, "So this is what you really think of Native people!" Then some time later, one reviewer referred to it as "witless white bashing." Evidently I have become a racist! (*Ibid.*)

And there is definitely some White baiting, if not White bashing, but I wouldn't call it entirely witless; Taylor is no Oscar Wilde, but he should share with Wilde, or any other playwright, the conceit of authorial distance any well-written play – or short story or novel – deserves from the outset. That is, if characters express outrageous, outlandish, racist, or otherwise controversial opinions, we should not assume that particular character is a mouthpiece for the writer, any more than a play or novel is a vehicle for the promotion of the writer's personal agenda.

Yet, although it is necessary for the audience to buy into such a writerly conceit, one would have to be terribly idealistic to believe that some literature and drama has not served as issue-driven sermon, propagandizing a person's or group's position. This is what drives Taylor's play. Each character, more or less, speaks from a particular ideology (including some hilarious *Star Trek* philosophy), some more eloquently than others, some more venomously than others. But has Taylor succeeded in creating largely unsympathetic characters? Or, has he created characters who deserve both scorn and sympathy? The latter would be the more successful reading, at least in terms of objective literary criticism. This play works on many levels, including the subjectivity of opinion. It is intended to poke fun, in a meaningful way, at a fractured debate, particularly the question of voice in art and academia, and Native literature in particular.

It may not be too great a stretch to argue that Taylor sees part of himself in each of the characters, with the exception perhaps of Michelle Spencer, the unflinching vegetarian who is the main target of the alterNative warrior – "a new breed of warriors who have an allegiance to the truth, rather than tradition" (Taylor 57) and the sarcastic s.o.b. Bobby Rabbit. His attacks on the strictness of that particular dogma and his joke-at-any-cost attitude contribute to the initial humour of the play and serve to fire up the emotions of the characters and catapult the evening's conversation into outright hostility. This eruption results in the exits of both host – Colleen Birk – and her guests. They are Yvonne Stone and the aforementioned Bobby Rabbit, the alterNative warriors and childhood friends of co-host Angel Wallace, and non-Native Michelle and her partner Dale Cartland. Only Angel, Ojibway science-fiction writer and ambiguous urban Indian, remains. That is until "innocently" ignorant Dale returns for more moose meat and conversation. The play closes with Dale, a fellow Trekkie and lover of sci-fi, looking past (or failing to see) the Native "issues" broached earlier in the evening, concentrating instead on Angel's writing, as Angel himself argued should be the case. But the story Angel closes with is certainly not devoid of "issue":

> There's this Native astronaut and he's cruising at the edge of the solar system in his space ship. And he's in a bad mood because back on Earth everybody is celebrating. The biggest party since... whenever, because the very last land claim has finally been settled... He picks something funny up on his scanners and goes to investigate. As he approaches the far rim of the solar system, in uncharted territory, he discovers a big space ... thing . . . The astronaut's sensors are going nuts . . . [G]radually, the thing understands that the astronaut speaks English and in translation the thing begins to spell out a message ... This big flashing thing suddenly says, in English, "For Sale." You get it, it's a huge interstellar billboard. Evidently the solar system is up for sale. The astronaut stares at it in disbelief.

> Then suddenly the sign slowly begins to change. It now says "Sold." Somebody's just bought the solar system. The Native astronaut mutters to himself "Not again." The end. (143-44)

Angel and Dale clink glasses and the lights go down. So, some of the ground covered in the play includes just that, ground, or land, and communication – or lack thereof.

The play, though, is not without its controversy. Racism, White guilt, appropriation, stereotype – these are not easy topics. As a mixed-blood scholar of Native literature, I read with both sympathy and something far less than scorn the character of Jewish Canadian professor of Native literature Colleen Birk. I realized from the outset the direction Taylor's play would take. I did not see this telegraphing as a fault of the play in my initial reading; rather, I was prepared to find my own position as both a scholar and person of mixed blood heritage challenged. And I like to believe I was up for the challenge, even if Colleen was not (although to be fair, she did not know she was entering such a charged arena – if that makes a difference). But the challenge is, nonetheless, deeply personal. Because of my "connection" to / interest in the so-called issues, I found myself wanting to pick sides but realized, ultimately, that although I've come to terms with my voice having a place within the discourse, that placement must be interrogated. The play doesn't pull any punches in this regard, although it starts slowly with Bobby referring to the bookshelf full of "Native" literature, including texts both by and/or about Aboriginal people:

> BOBB:. Hey Angel, nice collection of books. Yours?
> ANGEL: What do you think?
> BOBBY: I didn't think so.
> ANGEL: Colleen's.
> YVONNE: Wannabe?
> ANGEL: Literature professor.
> YVONNE: Almost as bad. Native Lit?
> ANGEL: Yeah.
> YVONNE: She any good?
> ANGEL: She has her strengths. (45-46)

From the outset, Angel's relationship with non-Native Colleen is destabilized. Although he has not derided her position openly, apart from jokingly putting her copy of *How a People Die* in the freezer ("Where else would you put a dead people but in a freezer?" 37), he has switched "allegiances" upon the arrival of his Ojibway friends. Or perhaps this is making too strong a case at this point, because allegiance is an issue of debate as well. Bobby and Yvonne see Angel's position – his relationship with a White woman, his disconnectedness from his past, his culture, his friends – as a change of allegiance. Angel feigns ambivalence, preferring to define his own identity, but his position – even his relationship with Colleen – is psychologically complicated, if we believe Bobby and Yvonne, and intentionally orchestrated. The penultimate revelation in the play, which serves as the impetus for the mass exodus of Colleen and her dinner guests, is that Angel orchestrated his meeting with Colleen months earlier because she interviewed Bobby and Angel for a book called *Legends of the Ontario Ojibway* when they were just children. Bobby and Angel had, of course, made up most of the stories. Bobby is thrilled, but Angel is deeply troubled by this fact. Angel says, "This book is in its seventh printing. This book is also on the reading list at five other universities that have a Native Literature course. Native teachers are teaching this book to Native students" (130). Bobby replies, "If it will make you happy, I promise I won't tell any more fake legends. At least not for fifty cents." To which Angel replies, "I just don't want to be an alterNative warrior any more. You've come to enjoy this too much. Too many people get hurt. As a result, they're missing your point . . . It's not the message I don't support, it's the medium" (131). And to Colleen he says,

> When I was seventeen, my Grandfather died. He had been a wonderful storyteller, and we had been very close . . . That night, after the funeral service, I had a dream. It was my Grandfather, he told me that about the importance of stories, of how often they're more important than the storyteller. He knew I had been up to mischief, and

> had not respected the art of storytelling. He told me I had to correct my mischief if I wanted to honour his spirit. I guess that's why I'm here. (136)

Colleen asks in disbelief, "Is that true?" and, narrowly avoiding some serious melodrama, Taylor has Angel reply, "No, but you were willing to believe it. Weren't you?" (137)

This exchange is the beginning of the end for Colleen and Angel and for the play. It is also, as a friend of mine – a Métis woman and fellow scholar of Native literature – pointed out in a conversation, the beginning of an even more problematic dynamic, one that all scholars and educators should be aware of when teaching Native literature: respect. Picking up on Yvonne's "wannabe" comment, Angel and Colleen have the following exchange when Colleen asks Angel if he still loves her:

> ANGEL: In Ojibway, how do you say "what time is it?"
> COLLEEN: What does that have to do with anything?
> ANGEL: I'll explain later. How do you say it?
> COLLEEN: I believe it's . . . aani epiijiyaag?
> ANGEL: And "I'm glad to meet you?"
> COLLEEN: This isn't the time . . .
> ANGEL: Humour me.
> COLLEEN: I'm glad to meet you. I think that's Nikichi-nendam nakweshkonaan. Does that humour you enough?
> ANGEL: One more. "I'm sorry."
> COLLEEN: Oh for Christ's sake . . .
> ANGEL: "I'm sorry."

> COLLEEN: Well that depends on who's sorry. And for what.
> ANGEL: I'm sorry.
> COLLEEN: Ndimijinwez.
> ANGEL: Now say those three sentences in Hebrew. I'll even accept Yiddish.
> *Colleen is silent.*
> ANGEL: I think that says it all. *[Beat.]*
> COLLEEN: Is it so wrong to want to share?
> ANGEL: I don't think that's sharing. You want to be more Native than I do. (137-39)

As my friend pointed out, while Angel may have a point, he, like Bobby, chooses to attack rather than engage in a discourse based on any healing principle. He has certainly failed to live up to the spirit of his admonishment of Bobby's "medium" or the spirit of truth at the heart of the alterNative warrior. Perhaps this is why he has rejected the movement. Earlier, Yvonne accused Colleen of being a "woman in search of a culture," saying, "You're Jewish, yet you're not. That explains you teaching Native literature. It's almost like you want to establish a connection to a culture to fill a vacuum" (112). Colleen's response then, which should still resonate with the listener/reader, especially after her final exchange with Angel, is "I am a Jew. I am proud of that. My personal connection to my people and religion are my business and not subject to your sophomoric psycho-babble" (113). However, after her exchange with Angel, it would appear that he considers her personal "connection" to Native literature as invalid because she is not Native, and despite her vast knowledge of culture and language, she is merely appropriating a culture to fill a void. This may be a standard form of the appropriation debate, but Angel's equation of her inability to speak Hebrew or Yiddish with a lack of respect for Native culture is flimsy logic. Perhaps, in the heat of the moment, Angel did not think out carefully what he wanted to say. There has been no mention of whether or not Angel speaks Ojibway, just that it is wrong that Colleen does. Maybe there is an unseen internalized debate raging here within Angel in which he asks of himself, What does it mean with regard to my identity as a Native person that I, unlike Colleen, cannot speak my own language?

My Métis friend and I found ourselves asking the same question, specifically in regard to our roles as scholars, students, readers and teachers. How would we respectfully teach a Native text, despite not having been raised on a reserve, learning "our" language(s) at our grandparents' knees? Taylor both perpetuates and questions stereotypes, ultimately asking what it means to be an authentic Indian. When I initially tried to make sense of *Daughters of Copper Woman,* I turned to Linda Alcoff's article, "The Problem of Speaking for Others," which addresses many of the problems prevalent in both postcolonial and feminist theory, with a particular focus on the study of Native literature. I was immediately struck by the simple (but not simplistic) and straightforward way in which Alcoff poses many probing questions regarding often contentious issues of authenticity and appropriation. She asks, "Is my greatest contribution to move over and get out of the way? And if so, what is the best way to do this – to keep silent or to deconstruct my discourse?" (8). As a young scholar, I was, like many young people, looking for a comfortable place to stand within the field of study, and trying to find the appropriate place for my voice. I found myself actively engaged in a deconstruction of my own discourse as well as some of the important questions encompassed by the title of Alcoff's article.

Although vastly different, both *Daughters of Copper Woman* and *Grey Owl* deal with the need to connect to a culture that is not one's own. These differences do not polarize the texts; rather, they serve to elucidate the ambiguous nature of connection and the need for the kind of discourse that questions what it uses and uses what it questions. Satya Mohanty writes, "What better way of ensuring the equality of cultures than to assert that, since all explanations of the other risk repeating the colonizer's judgements, we should simply refuse to judge or explain, forsaking understanding for the sake of respect" (111). Mohanty's comment is delivered with a sizable degree of irony and is the sort of problematization of issue that prompts Victoria Boynton to position herself as reader. I echo that declaration here because it rings true to my own sense of the problems with navigable/unnavigable boundaries and because it serves as a useful introduction to Anne Cameron's *Daughters of Copper Woman:* "I don't want to colonize through reading. I don't want to steal, appropriate, lay claim to what is not mine, impose what [Paula] Gunn Allen refers to as a "Western technological-industrial" mentality on the story, make a reputation off somebody else's culture" (Boynton 54). These are the two poles of my ideology, and my personal relationship to both Ruffo's *Grey Owl* and Cameron's *Daughters of Copper Woman* necessitates my need to similarly position myself as a reader.

I return to Linda Alcoff's article, "The Problem of Speaking for Others" because it offers a good set of parameters for such an engagement. Alcoff cautions against "retreating into an individualist realm" (21). She writes: "A further problem with the retreat response is that it may be motivated by a desire to find a method or practice immune from criticism. If I speak only for myself it may appear that I am immune from criticism because I am not making any claims that describe others or prescribe actions for them. If I am only speaking for myself I have no responsibility for being true to your experience or needs" (22). I could very well have qualified the preceding section on *alterNatives* with a statement amounting to an "in-my-opinion-and-my-opinion-alone-the-play-is-about . . ." as a pre-emptive deflation of criticism but that would have been as transparent as it is here. This is not to say that I believe my reading to be immune to criticism, just as I would expect some readers to disagree with Ruffo's decision to write about an impostor. Okanagan writer Jeannette Armstrong has been criticized and lauded for her use of a male title character in *Slash*. Patricia Morley, an early reviewer of *Daughters of Copper Woman,* called Cameron's text "a strong feminist statement [that] reminds us of a part of our history we have preferred to forget. Her work compels attention, calling out for social justice and spiritual healing" (43). But it remains appropriative. As a reader, perhaps as one who professes a "connection" to Native literature, perhaps as a man, this kind of reading, and Cameron's own statements that the stories in *Daughters of Copper Woman* are relevant to her, connected to her, because she is a woman, seems suspect. But Cameron is simply positioning herself.

Alcoff rejects a general retreat from speaking for others, but qualifies it, saying, "I am not advocating a return to an un-self-conscious appropriation of the other, but rather that anyone who speaks for others should only do so out of a concrete analysis of the particular power relations and discursive effects involved" (24). The parameter that is key to this discussion is the second in a list of four: "We must also interrogate the bearing of our location and context on what it is we are saying . . . One deformed way in which this is too often carried out is when speakers offer up in the spirit of honesty autobiographical information about themselves usually at the beginning of their discourse as a kind of disclaimer" (25). I have already engaged in just such an endeavour, although my positioning, vague though it was, cannot be said to be the sort of apology for being non-Native that Alcoff's definition alludes to. My claim of mixed heritage could be seen as an attempt to consciously occupy both insider and outsider positions (although we could argue which half is inside and which is out, depending on the forum). In this article it is more likely that the mixed claim will be seen as a not-so-subtle leaning toward insider Native status. I need not make such a claim, except that I have chosen to talk about the personal reading experience and what better way to inform such a subject? The paradox here, of course, is that in most discussions of non-Native literature, I would likely not make any such claim. In positioning myself I could simply be following the lead of many of the critics I have already quoted, as well as Julia Emberley in the introduction to her book, *Thresholds of Difference: Feminist Critique, Native Women's Writing, Postcolonial Theory,* and Cameron herself: "The question that gets asked most about [the book] is "Is this history or is this fiction?" Nobody ever stops to ask if the crap they push down your throats in school is history or fiction... this book, for me, as a person who was born on this island, and certainly as a woman, has more truth than anything the school system ever came up with" (Twigg 38). But is my positioning any different than Cameron's, articulated here in the preface to *Daughters of Copper Woman*?

> For years I have been hearing stories from the native people of Vancouver Island, stories preserved for generations through an oral tradition that is now threatened. Among the stories were special ones shared with me by a few loving women, who are members of a secret society whose roots go back beyond recorded history to the dawn of Time itself. These women shared their stories with me because they knew I would not use them without their permission. (7)

This last part is important and respectful, but it is likely the kind of statement Taylor is lampooning in *alterNatives*.

I study Native literature and culture because I want to connect with my Huron-Wendat ancestry, a connection that is made difficult by the fact that my maternal grandmother did not grow up in Wendake, the Huron-Wendat community in Lorrette, just outside of Quebec City. Even if she had, the strong traditionalist movement that I have come to know is relatively new. Add to that the literal distance between my long-established family home in Ottawa and the long-since-separated (in the Huron dispersal of 1650) Wyandot nations of Kansas, Oklahoma, Michigan, and Southern Ontario. And, while Bill C 31 retroactively reinstated status rights to those disenfranchised by earlier acts, it did not and could not by its very nature repair any of the real damage of severed connection. And, what of those people attempting to (re)connect, albeit with a respectful acknowledgement of vastly different experience? Where are the real rules and parameters that instruct people on how to connect or reconnect? This is precisely where individual decisions and experiences come into play, further blurring or greying lines of authenticity and appropriation.

It is out of a desire to show the proper amount of respect for that cultural heritage that I have imposed certain boundaries on myself, including an approach that, at times, is more academic than personal. Although that in itself has become a personal journey. I relate to Archie Belaney/Grey Owl, perhaps even envy him, and struggle with feelings of being an impostor, especially when confronted with questions of the hotly debated pan-Indian identity. That is why I felt such a connection to Ruffo's *Grey Owl*. But, when I first read *Daughters of Copper Woman,* I was similarly moved by Cameron's very powerful, compelling, and beautifully crafted narrative. I found myself asking difficult questions. What is my connection to a text that announces itself as being for women? What or who is it that I connect with – the Native subject matter or Anne Cameron, the White woman who, like Belaney, had access to a culture not her own? When my initial reaction was to say "White people can't do that" or "I wish a Native woman had written this," what was I really saying in regard to an already difficult discourse? When I read that the royalties from the book go not to Cameron but to the community from which she received many of the stories and that she did indeed "move over" when asked by a group of Native Canadian writers,[1] I found myself softening my initial negative reaction. I was thus forced to ask where my opinion fit into this whole mess and for the first time forced to consider the possibility that my opinion did not fit or matter at all, a telling admission for a male scholar discussing a decidedly feminist text.[2]

I initially embraced Cameron's book because of what it provoked in me as an academic. With the inherent objective distance of scholarship, I was able to say that Anne Cameron was wrong because appropriation is a philosophical issue, and she had appropriated what was not hers to use for her own means. Her end goal was not to promote Native women but to use them, to syncretize and primitivize. However, upon further research into the criticism of Cameron's work and the broader issues that necessarily developed, I began to see that my own struggle with the theme of the impostor was not far removed from issues of appropriation, authenticity and positionality. Many of Cameron's critics, Native and non-Native alike, have raised the issue of authenticity of voice. Christine St. Peter provides an interesting twist on the authenticity of genre: "On one level, *Daughters of Copper Woman* will only be considered authentic by ethnographers if Cameron has operated as a transparent medium, recording word-by-word transcriptions of Native stories" (503). And she adds, "I doubt that Cameron has done this, because the powerful filter of her own style appears to have given the stories their shape" (503).

St. Peter relates an anecdote that reveals the problems associated with *Daughters of Copper Woman*. "Many of the students in my women's studies course have insisted that this book was our most important reading, and they are suspicious of some local anthropologists who insist that Cameron has falsified the ethnographic tradition in her discovery of lost sources of female power. To their credit, the same students are disturbed to hear that some Natives also reject the book" (501). She rightly points out, however, that since many Native men and women admire it we can hardly reject it on their behalf. She asks, "If the writer is a woman intent on sharing knowledge of a hidden women's culture, can she assume a privileged position as transmitter for the sake of other women, even though not born to the racial heritage she recounts?" (501). This notion of accepting and/or rejecting is a privilege itself, and we must not lose sight of that. Alcoff concurs, saying that "we have to acknowledge that the very decision to move over or retreat can occur only from a position of privilege" (24). In fact, this discussion too is privileged insofar as it takes the form of a critical study of issue(s).

The point I am trying to make is that this is a worthy context in which to situate the teaching of *Daughters of Copper Woman*. However, in a classroom it may be more useful to turn this notion of privilege on its head and to re-use the word in another way: to make the point that it is a privilege to be welcomed into another's realm or sphere of experience and understanding. There is certainly an inherent "invitation" to engage in any published material. However, that material must be properly contextualized and interrogated. If we believe Cameron, she rightly and genuinely entered the circle of Native tradition because she was invited in, purportedly given permission to reproduce and interpret stories, and lastly, but no less importantly, because she is a woman. Some critics will see the use of the Kiki narrator/alter ego as a disguised (although not necessarily well-disguised) appropriative voice and statements like the following one by Granny as that sort of pre-emptive deflation of criticism. Cameron writes: "There's gonna be women jump up and start tryin' to make a religion out of it and tryin' to sound like experts and tryin' to feel big and look clever in front of other women. And they'll get tired after a while, and give up, but the truth will still be there for the ones who keep lookin' for it" (144). The truth is, it is not just women who have jumped at these stories, specifically to criticize. St. Peter is correct in her assessment of the situation. She says, "Different people hear differently; more pertinently here, different searchers – and this definitely applies to [Ron] Hamilton [a grandson of one of Cameron's primary informants] and Cameron" (502). She says of Hamilton that it can no longer be ascertained "to what extent he is defending his territory, or his grandmother's stories" (*Ibid*). The point is that it is his right to criticize and defend what he perceives as cultural appropriation or invasion. But his sphere of understanding does not encompass the whole of his grandmother's. There are portions that are unknown to him, but, and this is merely speculation for the sake of argument, perhaps not unknown to Cameron.

In another article, "Fringes, Imposture, and Connection: Armand Garnet Ruffo's *Grey Owl: The Mystery of Archie Belaney* and 'Communitist' Literature," I have written at length of Jace Weaver's notion of "communitism . . . a combination of the words 'community' and 'activism' " because literature "is communitist to the extent that it has a proactive commitment to Native community" (xiii). Again, speaking from the perspective of an engaged reader, that article discusses how *Grey Owl* serves a decidedly utilitarian purpose by thoughtfully examining the need to connect to a culture that is not one's own. Thus, in considering the positioning of Cameron in *Daughters of Copper Woman,* I now turn to Grey Owl in order to show how that text consciously addresses notions of cultural appropriation within the central theme of imposture, something *Daughters of Copper Woman* – without the proper contextualization – certainly lacks.

Growing up, I knew Grey Owl in the same way that I knew my Huron-Wendat great-grandfather: through photographs. In Grey Owl's case, there was the famous Karsh photo that hung in the Chateau Laurier's Karsh collection. As for my great-grandfather, there were the many pictures my family had of him. And, like Grey Owl, there were also the many newspaper articles, for he had had a somewhat public profile as Prime Minister Louis St. Laurent's personal aide; he had been known as the Indian who accompanied a Prime Minister around the world. The photographs were, as my family often said, unmistakably Indian; he was, in fact, lovingly referred to as the Cigar Store Indian whenever someone attempted to describe him without the aid of those photographs. But I never saw the Cigar Store Indian in him. He was always the gentleman wearing a three-piece suit in those photos. A wholly costumed Grey Owl, on the other hand, seemed truly unmistakably Indian despite the fact that I knew he was not. He fit the stereotype.

It was this connection to the Grey Owl myth that initially drew me to Ruffo's book. Having read many of the biographies, I was anxious to read a Native perspective. I was pleasantly surprised by Ruffo's approach. As a child I remember struggling with the problem that, though a fraud, Grey Owl had made the transition I could only imagine – to go Indian. That was my first, childish approach to connection to culture. Ruffo hints at possibilities of finding a deeper connection to a culture one may be only tenuously connected to, and this a worthwhile avenue for Native and non-Native scholars alike, but, most importantly, for those readers who turn to literature by Native and mixed-blood Native Canadians for insight into so-called Nativeness. The article explores the important role Grey Owl plays for readers looking to understand their own feelings of imposture when attempting to connect to some aspect of Native culture. Was Grey Owl the ideal Indian, or was it his ability to "go Native" that is the ideal for contemporary Native and mixed-blood Native Canadians? Or, is the message more akin to the repeated offer of kinship proffered by Natives in Ruffo's Grey Owl: "Dance with us as you can" (146)?

Working with both archival records and the oral history of his own family's connection to Belaney, Ruffo reconstructs a historical figure in a text that is part fact, part fiction. Ruffo subtly subverts a historically problematic genre: the Indian autobiography or biography. While clearly not autobiography, *Grey Owl* readily employs the actual writings of Belaney/Grey Owl and others, but we are not meant to confuse Grey Owl, the object, as writing by Grey Owl or any other of the first person voices within the narrative. However, the prominence given to Grey Owl's writing in the first of the book's two epigraphs is meant to serve as a validation of his role as text-producer and rightfully places him "in the pantheon of nature writers . . . with Henry David Thoreau, John Muir, Aldo Leopold, and Rachel Carson" (Brower 74). Ruffo's subversion of the Indian autobiography, while not necessarily overt to those unfamiliar with the history of Native literature as a distinct category, is evident on one basic level even before an engagement with the actual text. A quick glance at the author's bio and photo immediately following the narrative's close allows one to pick up on the fact that in this case the author is Native and his subject is non-Native. While Louis Owens has been critical of this extra-textual departure with regard to reviews of his own novels, saying "Do we really need to go beyond 'END' and consider photograph and bio blurb to decide the authenticity of a fiction?" (14), I argue that in this case it is a worthy exercise and one that adds, deliberately, to the flavour of the "mystery." The Native writing the story of the non-Native is an immediate send-up of the conventional early Indian biography, and, although Ruffo did not actually converse with Belaney for the book, he does employ excerpts from his journals and gives fictional voice to other undocumented events and so approximates what Arnold Krupat termed the "bicultural composite authorship" (262) or co-authoring of the Indian autobiography.

The Indian autobiography has essentially been ignored by literary scholars because, as Krupat notes, "[they] have been presented by the whites who have written them as more nearly 'scientific' documents of the historical or ethnographic type than as 'literary' works" (261) and do not conform to the accepted definition of autobiography as a narrative of a person's life written by that person. Krupat correctly notes that the Indian autobiography is a contradiction in terms. They are "collaborative efforts, jointly produced by some white who translates, transcribes, compiles, edits, interprets, polishes, and ultimately determines the 'form' of the text in writing, and by an Indian who is its 'subject' and whose 'life' becomes the 'content' of the 'autobiography' whose title may bear his 'name'" (262). On a very simple level, since the methodology of autobiography and even biography is limited to the telling of a story, the distance between the White culture's definition of history and a Native definition of history insofar as it applies to these genres should not be too great. After all, the exchange of personal "histories" is an integral part of Native cultural interaction. For example, a traditional greeting ceremony between the Mohawk and Ojibway nations would necessarily involve the exchange of stories that make up each respective group's history. However, because Native cultures do not see history as necessarily progressive and linear or "evolutionary, teleological, or progressive" (Krupat 261) and did not traditionally engage in a written tradition of recording stories as empirical data, the Indian "autobiography" is flawed at its roots because it cannot convey the necessary sense of mutability of story and even personal history. Krupat's essay concerns itself with the importance of treating the traditional Indian autobiography as literature rather than science and it is an important point. His principle of bicultural composite authorship at least acknowledges that there was a Native voice despite its diminishment through translation and transcription and the culturally biassed notion that the story of one's life as told by oneself (whether independently or in conjunction with another) can be used as historical fact. Whether White or Native, though, the voice can only approximate a perspective.

This issue of voice is an important one to Ruffo's *Grey Owl* because Archie Belaney as Grey Owl was the Native voice in the 1930s, at least to the White world on whose fringes Indians remained. His was an accepted point of view. And although not truly Native, he is essentially the embodiment of Krupat's bicultural composite authorship even though he did not work in conjunction with someone who actually belonged to the culture he spoke of – unless we count his relationship with Ruffo's family at Biscotasing and his numerous relationships with women of Native heritage. His life as Grey Owl had no ethnographical or anthropological significance because it was a fiction. As history, too, it is flawed because it necessarily demands that one choose a perspective. In this way, Belaney/Grey Owl, despite the openness with which his fraud is treated by Ruffo, is treated historically in much the same way as many famous Native North Americans. Consider the stories of Geronimo, Sitting Bull, or Cochise, whose words Belaney memorized as a child (2). Only until recently with the advent of revisionist movements, the kind that would see the influential Canadian poet Duncan Campbell Scott as a racist assimilationist and necessitate a re-examination of his poetry (specifically his "Indian" poems), have these stories been told from a Native perspective.

While there was considerable scandal concerning Belaney's unmasking – "*London Times, April 21, 1938* / Since the death of Grey Owl / a remarkable conflict of opinion / has arisen over his parentage, / particularly regarding his Indian blood" (Ruffo 207) – he has been treated relatively kindly by history, even by those who insist on concentrating on his ruse. Consider the excerpts from news reports that Ruffo closes with: "*Ottawa Citizen, April 20, 1938* / The chances are that Archie Belaney could not / have done nearly such effective work for conservation / of wildlife under his own name. It is an odd commentary, / but true enough ... *Liverpool Daily Post, April 21, 1938* / What, after all does his ancestry matter? / The essential facts about his life are not in dispute, / for as a conservation officer under the Canadian / Government, and as a lecturer and broadcaster / in Great Britain, he worked unceasingly for / the protection of wild life ... *Winnipeg Tribune, April 23, 1938* / His attainments as a writer and naturalist will survive / and when in later years our children's children / are told of the strange masquerade – if it was / a masquerade – their wonder and their appreciation / will grow" (207). This last passage is particularly telling and no surprise that Ruffo ends with it. It is surprising, however, that the conservative *Winnipeg Tribune*, like the *Ottawa Citizen* and London Times, should justify his fraud at all, but not surprising that they do so in this manner. His deception is acceptable, they imply, because it was for a good cause. Only the *Winnipeg Tribune* alludes to what Ruffo has similarly been alluding to all along: "if it was a masquerade" or, more succinctly put, it was simply a masquerade. Now, of course, this passage has been taken out of context and the original did not have the benefit of some sixty years of hindsight, but the reference to "children's children" is important. Ruffo is one of these children, as it was his great-grandparents' families that "adopted" Belaney. However, the newspaper article's reference to children was likely to those of its White readership and not inclusive of Natives. Throughout, Ruffo has subverted this and has made the last line a link to the Grey Owl epigraph that opens the book:

> The Trail, then, is not merely a connecting link between widely distant points, it becomes an idea, a symbol of self-sacrifice and deathless determination, an ideal to be lived up to, a creed from which none may falter. (ii)

Within the context of its original, this reference to "the trail" is a concrete one, although it is certainly mystified by Grey Owl. Here, though, as the textual introduction to Ruffo's narrative, it must be read in a different light. The fact that the word connection appears here is immediately significant, and the trail as symbol of the need to find one's way between two points – places, states of being – resonates heavily within the text where this subject matter is more overtly verbalized. Even the use of the word "distant" carries weight. It echoes the distance Krupat notes exists between the White and Native cultures.

Like Krupat's definition of the Indian autobiography, Grey Owl's life and writing live up to the notion that, as Bill Ashcroft et al. write, "the text creates the reality of the Other in the guise of describing it, [and] although [it] cannot operate as ethnography . . . the literary text . . . is not the site of shared mental experience and should not be seen as such" (59). However, Ruffo's narrative, despite spending little time on Belaney's life within the Native community at Biscotasing, subtly works to show the kinship between Belaney's perception of the Indian and Ruffo's own. This is accomplished by Ruffo's piecing together of authentic Belaney/Grey Owl writings and fictionalizing others. Except in Belaney's own mind, the severity of his fraud is never truly played out within the narrative. One would assume that his fraud would elicit a much stronger response from both the Native and non-Native camps. One might at least expect Native groups to have voiced concern as it is made clear by Ruffo that "an Indian can tell who's Indian" (128). But Ruffo takes a distinctly different direction with *Grey Owl* in two sections, both titled "John Tootoosis, 1936": "An Indian can tell who's Indian. / Grey Owl can't sing or dance. / But he's doing good / and when we meet / I call him brother" (128) and, later:

> We know Wa-Sha-Quon-Asin is not born of us, and we say nothing. For us it is of no importance. We do not waste our words but save them, because we know in this struggle of generations they are our strongest medicine. The man flies for us true and sharp, and we are thankful he has chosen our side. While we cheer, and the elders nod in approval, we can see the light shine in his face. We can see he feels better about himself than before. This is good. This is how it should be, to feel good about your-

self and your duty in the honourable way. Wa-Sha-Quon-Asin, we say, dance with us, as you can. (145-46)

Voice is further complicated by an extra-textual, untitled poem that follows the book's two epigraphs but precedes the section titled "Beginning"; it contains the first example of Ruffo's use of the second-person, "you," which here seems not to be an address to the implied reader as within the text but rather to a writer, historian, storyteller that may or may not be Ruffo. It begins:

> Archival memory.
> Paper brittle as autumn, unearthed
> across the desk, files scattered.
> Words floating like smoke
> smell of moccasins you are wearing
> warming the bright neon,
> carrying you on
> to the beginning
> It is past midnight, everyone
> is gone, except uniformed security
> and you – What is it you are digging for exactly? (iv)

This is an interesting decision by Ruffo, who is otherwise absent in the tradition of the biographer or Krupat's autobiographer. Clearly, though, we are meant to see that there is a connection between author and subject. When that unspecified narrator says "one day / you will catch him"(6), the "you" could apply to anyone who has been introduced to the Archie Belaney/Grey Owl mystery and who has seen the photograph of Archie as a child, or to this persona in charge of putting together the story. Similarly, when Grey Owl says, "You in the audience who sit in expectation cannot know. / This fear, this inexorable fear, I take with me" (104), the address could be to the implied reader of his journals or could be seen to be working on another level, with Ruffo, or the narrator of that prefacing poem, again addressing his implied reader. The real, historical connection between Ruffo and Belaney and a story about Belaney's need to connect with the culture of Ruffo's heritage is a complicated and cleverly disguised examination of his own or any connection to cultural heritage. His ambiguous address to an unspecified "you" allows other like-minded readers to explore the troubling issue of connection to Native heritage. A truly cultural component exists, then, to Krupat's bicultural composite authorship. Ruffo has made the making of Belaney's story his story. As such, this narrative line can be seen as an example of what Weaver defines as "the struggle to be self-defining" (44) in that Ruffo's use of Belaney's "history" as an exploration of a theme – connection to culture – speaks directly to a Native experience.

To many young people of Native heritage, Grey Owl was more successful as an authentic Indian than they could ever imagine themselves to be. Of course, the question of authenticity is further complicated in that Grey Owl is part of Ruffo's heritage; it was his Ojibway family that "adopted" Belaney. Why should he, then, or we, not look to Grey Owl as both a professional and cultural example? The answer for both may be because Belaney was an impostor. But it is this notion of impostor that Ruffo deconstructs. That feeling of not belonging or being an impostor is a real and valid emotion that contemporary Native writers deal with regularly, particularly with regard to the mixing of White and Native cultures and the issue of mixed cultural backgrounds.

We can complete the circle here with a return to Drew Hayden Taylor and his "Pretty Like a White Boy," a personal essay that deals with the difficulty of growing up as a status Indian who looks White:

> In this big, huge world, with all its billions and billions of people, it's safe to say that everybody will eventually come across personalities and individuals that will touch them in some peculiar yet poignant way. Individuals that in some way represent and help define who you are. I'm no different, mine was Kermit the Frog. Not just because Natives have a long tradition of savouring frogs' legs, but because of his music. If you all may remember, Kermit is quite famous for his rendition of "It's Not Easy Being Green." I can relate. If I could sing, my song would be "It's Not Easy Having Blue Eyes in a Brown Eyed Village."
> (436)

While I may be guilty of continuing the cycle of turning every issue into a philosophical debate by using *Daughters of Copper Woman* and its peripheral issues as pieces in a larger puzzle, there is a personal investment in this endeavour. Others may find varying degrees of use for such a discussion, in the same way that my symbolic connection to Grey Owl pales (pun intended) in comparison to Ruffo's own. What I have tried to illustrate is the difficult and ambiguous nature of connection. No matter how useful my model is, it still is limited in its scope. It does not allow me, my mother, or my grandmother to navigate the boundaries imposed by ourselves or by others any easier. What I have come to realize is that I am beginning to become comfortable "moving over" when my circle of experience and understanding no longer overlaps those that inform a particular discourse. So, rather than being an unconscious (or, more dangerously, a conscious) decision to act from a position of privilege, it is a respectful act. That does not mean it is a permanent action. If anything, it is simply a resistance to give in to the impulse to "teach rather than listen" (Alcoff 24). These are hard lessons to be learned from an even more difficult, but rewarding, obstacle course. While of extreme importance to know one's own position and positionality, it is as necessary to know and attempt to understand others', and not just to survive one of Angel and Colleen's dinner parties.

Notes

1 Lee Maracle makes a similar demand in her article "Moving Over." See Works Cited.
2 Again, Alcoff's parameters are extremely useful. The other three are: "1. The impetus to speak must be carefully analyzed and, in many cases (certainly for academics!), fought against . . . 2. Speaking should always carry with it an accountability and responsibility for what one says . . . 3. In order to evaluate attempts to speak for others in particular instances, we need to analyze the probable or actual effects of the words on the discursive and material context" (25-6).

Works Cited

Alcoff, Linda. "The Problem of Speaking for Others." *Cultural Critique* 20 (Winter 1991-92): 5-32.

Ashcroft, Bill, Gareth Griffiths, and Helen Tiffin. *The Empire Writes Back: Theory and Practice in Post-Colonial Literatures*. London: Routledge, 1989.

Boynton, Victoria. "Desire's Revision: Feminist Appropriation of Native American Traditional Stories." *Modern Language Studies* 26 (Spring/Summer 1996): 2-3, 53-71.

Brower, Kenneth. "Grey Owl." *Atlantic Monthly* (Jan. 1990): 74-80.

Cameron, Anne. *Daughters of Copper Woman*. Vancouver: Press Gang, 1981.

Dewar, Jonathan R. "Fringes, Imposture, and Connection: Armand Garnet Ruffo's *Grey Owl: The Mystery of Archie Belaney* and 'Communitist' Literature." *Creating Community: A Roundtable on Canadian Aboriginal Literatures*. Brandon, Manitoba: Bearpaw, 2001.

Emberley, Julia V. *Thresholds of Difference: Feminist Critique, Native Women's Writings, Postcolonial Theory*. Toronto: U of Toronto Press, 1993.

Krupat, Arnold. "The Indian Autobiography: Origins, Type, and Function." *Smoothing the Ground: Essays on Native American Oral Literature*. Ed. Brian Swann. Berkeley: University of California Press, 1983. 261-282.

Maracle, Lee. "Moving Over." *Trivia* 14 (Spring 1989): 9-12.

Mohanty, Satya. "Colonial Legacies, Multicultural Futures: Relativism, Objectivity, and the Challenge of Otherness." *PMLA* 110(1) (January 1995): 108-118.

Morley, Patricia. "Daughters of Copper Woman." *Quill & Quire* 48 (February 1982): 43.

Owens, Louis. *Mixedblood Messages: Literature, Film, Family, Place*. Norman, OK: University of Oklahoma Press, 1998.

Ruffo, Armand Garnet. *Grey Owl: The Mystery of Archie Belaney*. Regina: Coteau, 1996.

St. Peter, Christine. " 'Woman's Truth' and the Native Tradition: Anne Cameron's *Daughters of Copper Woman*." *Feminist Studies* 15(3) (1989): 499-523.

Taylor, Drew Hayden. *alterNatives*. Burnaby, BC: Talonbooks, 2000.

——. "Pretty Like a White Boy: The Adventures of a Blue Eyed Ojibway." *An Anthology of Canadian Literature in English*. 2nd ed. Ed. Daniel David Moses and Terry Goldie. Toronto: Oxford University Press, 1998. 436-439.

Twigg, Alan. "Nanaimo's Favorite Daughter: Eloquent and Immovable." *Quill & Quire* 48 (June 1982): 38.

Weaver, Jace. *That the People Might Live: Native American Literatures and Native American Community*. New York: Oxford University Press, 1997.

Addendum: July 2005

In the preceding article, originally published in Armand Ruffo's *(Ad)dressing Our Words: Aboriginal Perspectives on Aboriginal Literatures,* I wrote of the usefulness of certain texts in explorations of identity – particularly native and non-native schisms, mixed heritages, and racial versus cultural identity – and highlighted Drew Hayden Taylor's *alterNatives* as one such text. I found it useful personally and as a "teaching" tool. But really bringing this kind of text – one that challenges our assumptions – to the university classroom should be commonplace; it is not, though, as many of us know.

When one does find its way into the hallowed halls of academia, we should expect a raucous philosophical debate. At least, that's what our parents are paying for, right? But what happens when this play plays out in Aboriginal Canada, at the community level, far removed from literary, cultural or postcolonial studies, where such disciplines are unheard of or unimportant? Taylor, in his introduction to the play, writes of the mixed reactions he received from Native readers/audiences. Similarly, in a 2004 interview with Nunavut's *Nunatsiaq News,* Taylor relates the story of a particularly strong reaction. *Nunatsiaq News* writes, "One theatre company in Vancouver received a bomb threat from an outraged theatre-goer who didn't like 'plays that are racist against white people. I got a bomb threat and I thought that was so cool,' Taylor says." He goes on to echo the introduction to his play: "The white characters take a lot of abuse and the Native characters give a lot of abuse ... I've had at least two Native people come up to me after seeing this play and say 'is that what you really think about Native people?' It's really interesting to see who picks up on what."

The *Nunatsiaq News* interview was no accident. It was the result of a happy set of coincidences. I moved to Nunavut in 2001 to do research, work and get a finer appreciation of Inuit culture, after having spent most of my short academic career focused on Métis and First Nations issues. Along the way, I – and a like-minded group of volunteers – started the Qaggiq Theatre Company (originally the Qik Theatre Company). Our goal was, at least, to bring community theatre to Iqaluit and, perhaps, all of Nunavut. With a lifelong and very personal interest in Aboriginal issues – identity issues among them – and as the company's executive director, I helped shape the company's mandate to use the literary and performing arts as a tool to give young people a voice to explore their culture and the issues they face, particularly social issues.

In the spring of 2004, two acquaintances approached me to discuss doing a community production that summer and asked if I had any suggestions. Selfishly – and a little mischievously I'll admit – I suggested *alterNatives,* with the caveat that I thought it would be challenging, both because we had very little time to prepare for such a "talky" piece, but also because of its subject matter. To my delight, Erin Brubacher also knew the play and thought it was a great idea. We had several thoughtful discussions about the play and its issues and Brubacher and Odile Nelson, as co-directors, forged ahead, with Qaggiq producing.

I now turn the bulk of this addendum over to the driving forces behind this production, through interviews I recently conducted with Brubacher – a non-Inuk – and star (as Angel Wallace) Vinnie Karetak for this article. Taylor himself told *Nunatsiaq News* that the "issues involved are universal: interracial marriage, the concept of cultural appropriation, political correctness... Many Native issues are cross-cultural." But how would the cast and crew of Qaggiq's alterNatives handle the further twists of presenting an Ojibway playwright's work about First Nations characters in Inuit country?

*

Brubacher: It felt right to perform *alterNatives* in Iqaluit. In some ways, the cultural specificity of the Ojibway/white dichotomy in the play could be applied to any two cultures or ways of seeing. The play deals with universal issues of identity and colliding worlds: issues that are extremely relevant in Nunavut.

Karetak: I had never heard of Drew Hayden Taylor prior to the play. The first time I read the play, it was more or less to get a feel for it. I'm glad that both Erin and Odile had brought it up to the group. I was cast as Angel before I even read the play. It was really easy to relate to him as a character. I think that regardless of being Native or non-Native stories are universal across the country, so this play was easy to relate to.

Brubacher: *alterNatives* is a play that asks who we are, who we're allowed to be and how we might choose to be whatever we want. We faced these same issues when casting the play: it would have been impossible, in a northern community of six thousand, to find a Jewish woman to play Colleen, or three Ojibway actors to play Angel, Yvonne and Bobby. More to the point, we weren't interested in finding actors who shared their characters' race, culture, or even gender. I had no desire to see three white Iqaluit residents play Colleen, Michelle and Dale and three Inuit play Angel, Yvonne and Bobby. It would have implied that all first people are the same, like saying: Ojibway, Inuit, what's the difference? This kind of a casting decision would have been a huge mistake.

We thought about doing the reverse and having whites play the Ojibway characters and Inuit play the whites – just so there was a visual difference between the two groups – but that also felt really wrong; too heavy-handed, like we were trying to make some kind of statement we weren't. So in the end we chose actors who were best suited to the parts, in voice, personality and feeling. We even decided to have a woman play Bobby: she was the best person to play that part. Nobody played a role into which they were born. Drew Hayden Taylor's writing allowed us to do this because all identifying marks were already in the script. That's the magic of the theatre; an Inuk woman can stand on a stage in Iqaluit and say: "I am an Ojibway man at a dinner party in Toronto," and we'll believe him.

Karetak: Although we are different people, First Nations, Métis and Inuit have lots in common in terms of being a minority. The identity issues might be understood by any minority group.

Brubacher: The more we came to know the play, the more we found that the decisions we made in casting alterNatives complemented the questions raised by the play itself. Because while it's impossible for someone born into one experience to ever fully understand the experience of "the other," that doesn't negate the importance of trying; something Dale and Angel show us over a moose roast with a side of science fiction, and something that all the actors in this production tried as they struggled to understand the culture of each character without assimilating the stereotypes that the play already exposes.

Karetak: The humour was crucial in this play. It made non-natives laugh at themselves, it made natives laugh at themselves. So it was easy to not feel bad at laughing at the "other side." It brought everyone together or put them on the same page. Nothing is sacred, everything and everyone is game to being made fun of.

Brubacher: I don't think there are any villains or heroes in *alterNatives*. Taylor makes fun of everybody. But you can also really feel for all the different points of view this play presents. You get the sense that they are all somehow well intentioned and misguided. They all do/say really hurtful things and they are all wounded. Much of this underlies the humour and I think that's a good thing. The comedy during the play allows the sharper, more important issues to linger later. It allows the audience to think about all the questions raised by the play and to come to their own conclusions, rather than being spoon-fed answers by the playwright.

Karetak: The production of the play, I thought, went really well. It was a crazy five weeks. I still can't understand how we managed to pull it off with almost all of us working full-time jobs. I don't recommend anyone put a show together in that amount of time. I'm glad that we did it though.

★

I'll close with an excerpt from an unpublished interview I conducted with Joe Osawabine, Artistic Director of De-ba-jeh-mu-jig Theatre Group, a Manitoulin Island-based First Nations company Qaggiq Theatre has worked with and to whom we are indebted for their generous mentoring. Shortly after we wrapped up *alterNatives,* I asked Joe how De-ba-jeh-mu-jig handles the identity issue in their work, and I think his answer should also be taken into the classroom — especially where texts and performance pieces by Aboriginal artists are being taught (dissected?) and where Aboriginal and non-Aboriginal students might find themselves in discussions of Aboriginal identity.

Osawabine: I feel that we as artists must be comfortable in our own identities as [Aboriginal] people before we can even begin to express our identity as an art form. Once we are comfortable in our own skin then we can take the stereotypes that have been labeling us for many years and have much more ownership over them, as a way to overcome them. At De-ba-jeh-mu-jig we are a fairly mixed group of people on a cultural level, as our artists and interns come from across the country. Plains Cree, Ojibway, Tlingit, Odawa, Pottawatami, Inuit, as well as half-breeds and full-bloods (or at least as full as one can get these days) are all represented within the company. So at any given time we may have a person of other cultural background playing an Ojibway character. Often times when creating our work, the background of the person has very little to do with the character on stage. I don't mean to say that it is disregarded, just that we are what we are and I don't have to keep reminding myself that I am playing an "Ojibway" character; it's just ingrained in the fact that I am ... and the cultural expression/impression that comes with that will come out naturally in the way I play the character. Also, because we live and work on a reserve, on an Island, in Northern Ontario, instead of on John Street in Toronto, our entire community context and ecology is culturally appropriate. Your native identity is seldom questioned when you live on a reserve! The relevant question may be "Does the actor performing the role understand and inhabit an Aboriginal World View?" If yes, he/she will be convincing even if he/she looks Chinese. After all, we have black status Indians living on reserve here. It is not about looks, it is about how you see and experience the world, and how you fit in to it.

★

Qaggiq Theatre Company's first Inuit legend production is underway with a local premiere planned for Fall 2005, starring Karetak and several other Inuit actors, dancers, singers and artists. But the production is also an amalgam of the talent available in Nunavut. It is mostly Inuit. It is mostly Aboriginal, with some members of other Aboriginal groups from North and South America, but not entirely so. Ultimately, it is about art and culture, culture and art. These young artists will tell a version of a centuries-old story, one that exists in different versions across the circumpolar world, and it may be very different from that of some audience members. Are these artists "alterNative Warriors" in search of the Truth or practitioners of the

"Selective Traditionalism and the Emergence of the Narrow-Focused Cultural Revival" school of thought? Or neither? We may wish to take a page from the worldview of Drew Hayden Taylor: *Bring on the debate! (But maybe not the bomb threats . . .)*

Works Cited

Minogue, Sarah. "On stage: AlterNatives serves up cross-cultural confection," *Nunatsiaq News,* July, 9, 2004. (available online at: http://www.nunatsiaq.com/archives/40709/news/nunavut/40709_08.html)

Osawabine, Joe. Personal interview. 2004.

The Spiritual Tourist in The Plays of Drew Hayden Taylor

Kristina Fagan

At the beginning of Drew Hayden Taylor's play, *The Baby Blues,* a young white woman appears on the stage, wearing heaps of turquoise and beaded jewelry, carrying a tape recorder, and overflowing with enthusiasm:

> . . . I'm here at an actual, real-life pow wow! Oh, how beautiful, simply so beautiful. Just smell that wood smoke, the bacon frying – what a pity I don't eat meat. Oh, listen to the children of nature playing, being one with the lake. Oh, it is bliss, sheer bliss. The harmony I feel in this place. Here I am, surrounded by trees, flowers, grass, squirrels, and Native People. Tree to tree, First Nations. Aboriginal people in their natural environment. Indigena everywhere! Oh, I hope I have the honesty and spirit to open myself up to these people and show them my purity of heart so they will accept me into their fold. These people have so much to teach us. (11-12)

This character, who calls herself Summer, is immediately recognizable as a type found at many Aboriginal cultural events, a type that I call the "spiritual tourist." Western society, having widely rejected the demands of its own religious traditions, has been looking more and more for a sense of meaning in the religious traditions of "other" –

usually Eastern and Aboriginal – cultures. Yet the spiritual tourist typically lacks the historical knowledge and community context to make sense of these traditions, and so ends up depending on stereotypes and commodified symbols or objects – miniature Zen gardens, dream-catcher earrings, meditation tapes, sweat lodge workshops, etc. It is easy to ridicule the spiritual tourist; when I saw a production of *The Baby Blues,* Summer got a lot of laughter from the audience even before she opened her mouth. However, the tourist is not the only participant in this industry; spiritual tourism is often encouraged by people from the "other" culture who are more than willing to accept the advantages that tourists may offer. In *The Baby Blues* and its sequel, *The Buz'Gem Blues,* Drew Hayden Taylor explores the problems with spiritual tourism, and none of the characters involved, white or Aboriginal, escapes his critical and satirical eye.

The character of Summer is a representative of a large consumer desire for Aboriginal spirituality. Virtually every Canadian airport gift-shop carries an array of dream-catchers, carvings of Inuit shamans, braids of sweetgrass, etc. As an example of the way that spiritual tourism industry works, consider an advertisement that the Canadian government published in the *New York Times,* encouraging affluent New Yorkers to visit the West Coast of

Canada. The headline of the ad immediately announces that British Columbia is a spiritual place: "Only in God's Country Could You Meet Such Interesting Souls." Below this is a large photograph of three (presumably Aboriginal) people on a beach. Two are wearing large raven masks while a third emerges from the mist carrying a ceremonial drum. The accompanying text begins: "While Canada's Pacific coast is still undiscovered by many of this world, our native people have been entertaining visitors for centuries" and goes on to use the Haida creation story to promote British Columbia as a place where "the supernatural abides in all that is living."[1]

This advertisement reveals many of the problems with spiritual tourism. For one, it draws on and contributes to a stereotype of Aboriginal people as exotic, natural, and spiritual — as both more and less than ordinary human beings. Tourists attracted to British Columbia by this ad would probably be disappointed to see that most Aboriginal people in Canada wear jeans much more often than ceremonial masks and are more likely to be found watching television than wandering around on misty beaches. It also commodifies West Coast Aboriginal people — note the use of the phrase "our native people" — and their sacred traditions and stories. Furthermore, its optimistic claim that Aboriginal people have been "entertaining" for centuries, conjuring an image of dancing Natives inviting the settler-invaders onto their land, glosses over the much darker history of Native-Newcomer relations on the West Coast.

Not surprisingly, there is a long history of Aboriginal people laughing at such depictions and at the tourists who buy into them. Most of the time, such jokes about tourists are not made in the presence of whites (Basso 31). Keith Basso's 1979 *Portraits of the "Whiteman"* was an unusual exception, documenting his observations of how the Apache mockingly imitated white tourists' loudness, pushiness, and insensitivity. More recently, however, Aboriginal writers have brought such humourous depictions of tourists to the general public.[2] But while many Aboriginal writers have touched on the spiritual tourism phenomenon, Taylor is arguably the one who has given it the most sustained examination, looking at the issue in several plays; he explores the issue in greatest detail through the character of Summer in *The Baby Blues* and *The Buz'Gem Blues*.[3]

Through Summer, Taylor examines the desire for spiritual tourism. Summer, whose real name, we eventually discover, is Agnes Ducharme, seems unwilling to accept her own background or identity. She does not claim her real name or her real heritage (French), instead focusing on developing a persona based on her tiny portion of Native blood. However, she does not know from which Nation that one sixty-fourth comes and so focuses on generalized symbols of "Indianness" – wearing Aboriginal jewelry, making frequent references to the Creator, and learning an impressive variety of Aboriginal languages. She admits that she is drawn to Aboriginal people because she feels that they have something she feels that she lacks: "It's your sense of belonging. You know who you are, where you come from" (*Buz'Gem* 66). Here, Taylor hints that non-Aboriginal people in North America lack a clear sense of their own home and history, and therefore seek a sense of belonging through others.

Lacking in self-awareness, Summer is equally oblivious to other people. She is unaware of others approaching (*Baby* 12) and does not realize when people are angry with her (*Buz'Gem* 39), laughing at her (*Baby* 14), or taking advantage of her (*Baby* 15). This lack of sensitivity extends to her views of Aboriginal people. She un-self-consciously subscribes to all the stereotypes of Aboriginal people as uniformly wise and noble and she looks to them to satisfy her own desire for spiritual fulfilment. Throughout the two plays, Summer is searching for, as she explains, "a guide in my quest to understand the aboriginal spirit" (*Buz'Gem* 102) and she looks to each Aboriginal man that she meets to be that guide. She sees the men, not as equals with whom she could potentially have a partnership, but as sources of wisdom. Summer's apparent immediate willingness to enter into romantic relationships with the men also reveals how the desire for the exotic is linked to desire for the erotic (a theme that Taylor is now exploring in more detail through his work on Native erotica).

Summer's attitude towards Aboriginal people is explored in both plays through images of food and eating. "Ethnic foods" are probably the most popular tourist commodity — and, indeed, *The Baby Blues* is largely set at a snack bar where Amos sells typical pow wow fare — Buffalo Burgers, Indian tacos, corn soup, etc. Summer approaches the snack bar saying, "[G]ive me a Buffalo Burger and I will be proud to eat and digest it" (36). Here, the image of the tourist as a literal consumer suggests the metaphorical consumption of Aboriginal culture, especially when we consider that the arrival of Europeans meant the extinction of wild buffalo and consequently the destruction of the Aboriginal economy on the plains. Summer asks for a Buffalo Burger even though she does not usually eat red meat, revealing her perception of Aboriginal food as "different" (36). Taylor has cleverly combined the theme of food with the issue of spiritual tourism through Amos' specialty, Fortune Scones. Fortune Scones, actually a combination of bannock and Chinese fortune cookie, appeal to tourists' desire for "Native wisdom"; Amos comments wryly: "[I]t sells. White people will buy anything" (35). Summer is so delighted with her Fortune Scone, she exclaims, "I will treasure it forever" (64). Amos, however, encourages her to treat the scone as food: "If you want my advice, just eat the damn thing" (64). This interaction interestingly echoes a pow wow scene in Eden Robinson's "Queen of the North" in which a white spectator buying fry bread asks the protagonist Adelaine, "How should I eat these?" (208) and she thinks, in response, "With your mouth, asshole" (208). Both Amos's and Adelaine's responses assert that their foods (and, by extension, they) are normal and familiar, rather than exotic and "other."

Clearly, Summer is guilty of using and dehumanizing Aboriginal people. Taylor's critique of the selfish spiritual tourist is unmistakable. But it is important to remember that the Aboriginal men with whom she deals are not her passive victims. They are more than willing to serve as her "spiritual guides" (and sexual partners). This willingness, however, puts them into a difficult position, one that Aboriginal guides have been confronting for centuries. On the one hand, acting as a guide brings advantages – sometimes money or prestige, sometimes (as in Taylor's plays) sex appeal. Furthermore, a guide can potentially promote awareness of Aboriginal people and their spiritual traditions. But, on the other hand, a guide to spiritual tourists faces the dangers of self-stereotyping and of "selling" (more or less directly) sacred traditions. These are dangers which Aboriginal people have long negotiated.

As an example, consider the ways in which Aboriginal people dealt with that quintessential spiritual tourist, Edward Curtis. Early in the twentieth century, Curtis travelled around Western North America, taking thousands of photographs of Aboriginal people. The photographs, which showed solemn-looking Aboriginal people dressed in ceremonial clothing, both drew on and contributed to popular stereotypes of the "noble savage." In fact, Curtis went out of his way to ensure that nothing interfered with that stereotype; he carefully removed all traces of white influence from his photos and provided his own props to create the desired images. It would be easy to think of Curtis as exploiting the Native people he photographed, but that is only part of the story. Aboriginal people who remember Curtis have recounted that, rather than being passive objects, they and their people were active participants in Curtis's project. Anne Makepeace, who directed a documentary on Curtis, reports that many of his photographic subjects saw themselves as making a record of traditions that had been outlawed, a record that would be of value to their children and grandchildren. When they entered Curtis's photographic tent, they would put on their best regalia, wanting to be remembered as people of dignity who were still connected to their ancestors and to their traditions. They also maintained a sense of propriety and privacy, forbidding certain traditions and ceremonies to be photographed (Makepeace). And, despite the stoic expressions found in Curtis's photographs, elders recall that they found the unrealistic situations and poses into which Curtis put them quite funny (Makepeace). For example, in a 1915 sepia-toned photograph entitled "Hesquiat maiden," a young woman wearing a serious expression turns her head to the side, showing the elaborate cedar bark ornaments in her hair. The mood of the photo is serene and majestic. Yet Curtis's own notes tell a different story: "The girl wears the cedar-bark ornaments that are tied to the hair of virgins on the fifth morning of their puberty ceremony, as described in Volume xi, page 42. The fact that the girl who posed for this picture was the prospective mother of an illegitimate child caused considerable amusement to the native onlookers and to herself."[4] Suddenly, to me, the picture looks very different. The young woman is not an isolated figure, but is surrounded by teasing family and friends. I picture her trying not to laugh, the corners of her mouth twitching as she puts on a suitably noble expression. Curtis's photographic subjects used the three major strategies used by Aboriginal people in dealing with spiritual tourism. First, they used the tourism situation for their own purposes and gains. Second, they hid or refused access to certain aspects of their spiritual traditions. And third, they, fully aware of the absurdity of the situation, acted out the roles that Curtis wanted them to play.

In *The Baby Blues* and *The Buz'Gem Blues,* the Aboriginal characters use all three of these strategies — exploitation, concealment, and ironic role-playing — to deal with the demanding character of Summer. First, while Summer is trying to get something from the men, they are also trying to get something from her. The men in *The Baby Blues* — Skunk, Noble, and Amos — see Summer primarily as a sex object. Skunk gets her naked with promises of a "morning purification . . . [in] Mother Earth's lake" (15). Noble tries to seduce her with his storytelling, although the only story he can think of is "The Three Little Pigs" (44). And, at the play's end, she is romantically involved with Amos, the much older owner of the pow wow snack bar, who promises to teach her all about her (virtually non-existent) aboriginal heritage. The men also look to Summer for economic advantages: Noble plans to use her as a free ride out of town (*Baby* 65-68), while Amos uses her as free labour for his catering business (*Buz'Gem* 21-22).

While benefitting from Summer's spiritual tourism, the men also ensure that they do not reveal any important cultural or personal information for her consumption. The imaginary ceremony that Skunk invents, for instance, does not give Summer any actual sacred knowledge. Noble, similarly, lies about having been at Oka and Wounded Knee (*Baby* 40-41), carefully hiding his real life story. He never, for instance, lets her know that he has just found out that he is Pashik's father. This revelation, which forms the central plot of the play, happens virtually under Summer's nose without any other character telling her what is going on. And in *The Buz'Gem Blues,* Amos appears to share more of his personal history with Martha, whom he has just met, than with his girlfriend, Summer (95-98). Aboriginal guides have long been aware of the dangers of revealing too much. In the 18th century explorer David Thompson's journals, he recounts how his Cree guides, who had led him onto their land, and taught him their language and many of their stories, were nevertheless careful about how much of their culture they revealed. One day, Thompson heard them use their word for rainbow, a word with deep spiritual implications, and asked his guides why they had never taught him that word. They answered, "You whitemen always laugh and treat with contempt what we have heard and learned from our fathers, and why should we expose ourselves to be laughed at" (42). With Summer, the danger is not that she will laugh, but that she will tape-record, misunderstand, and appropriate as part of her own persona.

Rather than revealing anything about themselves or their own people, the men in *The Baby Blues* act out the stereotypes that Summer expects. For her, they play out the role of the wise and deeply spiritual Native. For instance, Noble gets Summer to come to his tent, saying, "I can tell you all about the spiritual meaning of my dances" (39). Even Amos, who appears to be the most honest of the male characters, takes advantage of Summer's perception of him as a wise elder (91) and explains his romantic relationship with Summer using uncharacteristically formal, strangely inappropriate, and perhaps parodically "wise words": "It's always been my belief that as long as there's one drop of Native blood in her, she's my daughter. And I will honour that" (92). It seems that his relationship with Summer is based so heavily on role-playing that he cannot even escape it when she is not present. Robert Nunn has usefully analyzed the men's "Native mimicry of white pronouncements on authentic Indianness" (110), showing how, by acting out Summer's (and some audience members') stereotyped expectations, the male characters interrogate and challenge those expectations.[5]

The men's treatment of Summer constitutes a powerful critique of spiritual tourism, one which, in addition to being entertaining, can serve as an education and even a warning for non-Aboriginal audience members. However, within the plays, we can see that the results of the men's strategies are ambiguous. Their ways of dealing with Summer give them, as discussed, certain concrete advantages, and also serve to protect them from her prying and demanding personality. But, on the other hand, the men's relationships with Summer are clearly unfulfilling and, one by one, they move on to relationships grounded in reality rather than in parody, Noble with his daughter, and Skunk with his new Aboriginal girlfriend. Amos, who maintains a relationship with Summer the longest, seems exhausted from dealing with her demands: "Ah Summer, you have so much to give. Why do you always have to give it to me?" (*Buz'Gem* 28). He is also quick to criticize her behind her back (*Buz'Gem* 97), and eventually leaves her for Martha, an Aboriginal woman with whom he can be himself. Tired of playing her "Elder of love" (*Buz'Gem* 25), it seems that Amos has reached the limits of mimicry. Other Native writers and artists have also depicted the difficulties of dealing with stereotypes through parody. In "Queen of the North," Adelaine is confronted by a white tourist willing to pay a hundred dollars for a plateful of bannock and a look at her long black hair. Well aware of the technique of parodying tourists' stereotypical expectations, Adelaine considers this approach:

> "What are you making?" . . .
> At the beginning when we were still feeling spunky, Pepsi and I had fun with that question. We said, Oh, this is fishhead bread. Or fried beer foam. But bull-shitting took energy.
> "Fry bread," I said. (206)

Perhaps the "bullshitting" of parody does take too much energy, requiring a constant state of self-disguise. Artist Carl Beam, who often uses stereotypes in his work, expresses the same feeling as Adelaide: "I can't be endlessly ironic because the irony goes two ways. There's a psychic price; it also implodes. Knowing the world is so shallow and stupid is emotionally draining" (qtd. 186). *The Baby Blues* and *The Buz'Gem Blues* both depict the "psychic price" for Aboriginal people engaged in the spiritual tourism industry.

For Summer, the price of spiritual tourism is arguably even higher. Each of the men's strategies – exploitation, concealment, and role-playing – has negative impacts on Summer. First of all, Summer (herself an exploiter) is exploited, lied to, and taken advantage of by the men in *The Baby Blues*. While, in a racist world, Summer undoubtedly has a racial advantage, when we consider the factors of age and gender, as well as Summer's gullibility and isolation at the pow wow, it is clear that she holds little power in her relationships with the men. Furthermore, the men's concealment of themselves behind an ironic façade ensures that Summer does not significantly change her limited ideas about Aboriginal people. In *The Baby Blues*, the men's ironic humour is recognized by one another and by the audience but never by Summer (39). To recognize irony requires a degree of knowledge that Summer lacks. Haida writer Marcia Crosby points out this problem in her discussion of a George Bowering novel that parodies Indian stereotypes: "The entrenching of the fictive stereotypical Indian, which is still perceived as real by many people because of the enormous body of texts and images which support that notion, negates the positive aspects of the form of writing Bowering chooses to use. One can only parody something that is shared, otherwise it's an 'in' joke" (90-91). Similarly, the men's parody of Summer's stereotyped expectations is an "in joke" among them; to Summer, the stereotypes are actually reinforced. When we reach the sequel, *The Buz'Gem Blues*, we can see that Summer, despite now being involved in a serious relationship with Amos, does not seem to have changed her limited view of Aboriginal people in any significant way. She still thinks everything Amos does should be "spiritual or ethno-based" (19). Amos and Summer have both been playing roles and, when the relationship amicably ends, we can see that it has not led to any personal growth or to improvements in Native–non-Native relations.

While Amos, Skunk, and Noble move on to more meaningful relationships (with other Aboriginal people), Summer's final relationship is more ambiguous. She becomes involved with The Warrior Who Never Sleeps, a young Cree man whose real name is Ted Cardinal and who hides behind a pair of sunglasses, spiritual mumbo-jumbo, and a warrior pose. The Warrior Who Never Sleeps is depicted as Summer's Aboriginal equivalent, desperately trying to prove his Aboriginality. Over the course of the play, both characters are convinced to shed their invented names and costumes and to try to be "who they really are." However, while we learn something of The Warrior's true self – he is actually a nerdy lover of *Star Trek* who decided that he needed to focus his life on something other than cable television – we never do learn anything about Agnes Ducharme's background except that she is French. Furthermore, while The Warrior is, by the end of the play, able to blend his warrior side with his Trekkie side, Summer's position is less clear. We see few signs at the end of the play that she is incorporating her French identity (except for a single "au revoir" (*Buz'Gem* 119)). While, at one point, she seems to be trying to "embrace her new reality" as Agnes Ducharme (99-102), she later says that that was a "false reality" (110). And she falls in love with the Warrior at the moment when they both revert to their old personas, crying "Free Leonard Peltier" and "Oka Forever" with raised fists (103). She listens with awe to his pseudo-spiritual babbling:

> WARRIOR: Today is a good day to find the first day of the rest of your life ... or something like that.
> SUMMER: Isn't he magnificent? (111)

It seems that, in The Warrior, Summer has found yet another "spiritual guide." She follows him to an Aboriginal *Star Trek* convention just as she previously followed Skunk, then Noble, then Amos. We are left wondering whether she has her own goals and whether she has truly developed at all. For Summer, as for the men, spiritual tourism seems to be ultimately unfulfilling.[6]

Taylor's plays paint a complex picture of spiritual tourism. Rather than simply criticizing the white tourist, he examines the dangers of spiritual tourism, both for the tourist and for the Aboriginal "guide." While such tourism might bring some personal gains, he suggests, it too often involves dishonesty, concealment, and the perpetuation of stereotypes. Furthermore, at least within these two plays, it does not seem to lead to better cross-cultural understanding or significant development of the white spiritual tourist.

This consideration of Summer then leads to the question: how can Aboriginal and non-Aboriginal people move beyond a tourist interaction to a meaningful relationship? Taylor's implicit answer to this question is expressed, once again, through images of food. Earlier in this essay, I discussed the way that Summer's approach to Aboriginal food is suggestive of her attitude toward Aboriginal people. In *The Buz'Gem Blues,* Summer is working for Amos, who is catering an Elders' conference. She is attempting to cook "cross-cultural foods," a symbol of her relationship with Amos. But the majority of Summer's recipes – Chocolate Moose, Salmon Shake, Macaroni and Tofu Soup, Cheese Manicotti with Cheese made from Caribou Milk, Western Sandwich made with Turtle Eggs – sound at best difficult to make and at worst unappetizing. In fact, her food makes Marianne sick (67) and Amos calls it "the culinary equivalent of Frankenstein" (91). It seems that Summer, while she likes the *idea* of these foods, has not actually bothered to taste them. She has not, in other words, used any aesthetic sense, what Amos calls "gut instinct": "Her recipes aren't working. I should have went with my gut instinct. *(patting his belly)*" (91). Analogously, Summer seems unable to simply enjoy her relationships with Aboriginal people because she has too many expectations and preconceived ideas. It is no surprise, then, that Amos prefers Martha, with whom he can create a decent meal and enjoy a can of Spam.

Summer's foil in The Buz'Gem Blues is Professor Savage, a white researcher who, throughout the play, has been trying to interview the Aboriginal characters about their "Courting, Love, and Sexual Habits" (12). Yet despite his interest in others' sexuality, he seems to have no sex life of his own, having only a cat for companionship. To his dismay, his research subjects keep turning the discussion back to his own intimate life (46, 77, 108, 118) and suggesting that he consider his own "pleasures." Marianne even uses the cooking analogy, suggestively asking the professor, "Do you just follow the recipe or do you cook by taste?" (118). Unlike Summer, however, the professor does seem to learn to "taste." By the end of the play, he admits that his tourism/research has been unsuccessful. Nevertheless, he adds, he did "find out that Ojibway women like being tickled" (125) through his new relationship with Marianne, and he has discovered a taste for Spam, which he is eating during his final speech. This scene echoes the ending of Taylor's play, *alterNatives,* in which an Ojibway and white man sit down together to enjoy a moose roast. Perhaps the suggestion of both endings is that the way for people to learn about each other is not through tourism, where one person seeks to "get something" from another, but through shared pleasures. And this pleasure, of course, extends beyond food to the pleasures of learning and of human companionship. Both plays, as Helen Hoy has written about Adelaine's "with your mouth" comment, "reaffirm the importance of gustatory and aesthetic pleasure ... Take delight in what you are offered. Taste what you are eating; don't just classify and anatomize it." (195). The major difference between Summer and Professor Savage is that we never do see her clearly move away from the one-sided tourist gaze and towards reciprocity in her relationships, towards sharing her own life story and taking simple pleasure in her interactions with others. In fact, after having traveled through two plays with her, we know virtually nothing of Summer's own background, tastes, or pleasures.

Summer's similarities to Professor Savage emphasize the connections between tourism and much of the scholarship on Aboriginal people. Indeed, there are significant similarities in the motivations and approaches of spiritual tourists and some white scholars. Aboriginal people have often criticized researchers for their brief visits to communities, their selfishness (using others for their own goals), their unremitting curiosity and pushiness, and their focus on material culture – all common characteristics of the spiritual tourist.[7] Helen Hoy has also made this link between the consumption of culture by both tourists and scholars in titling her recent monograph on Aboriginal literature *How Should I Read These?*, deliberately echoing the hungry tourist in Robinson's "Queen of the North." In fact, Taylor also makes the link explicit; Summer is an anthropology student working on her thesis. Her vocabulary – "I was raised as a member of the oppressive white majority" (*Baby* 13); "That was just my white concept of pan-Indianism coming through" (Baby 37); "I would love to hear your opinion on the socio-political implications" (*Baby* 41) – clearly identify her as a scholar (or perhaps a wannabe scholar), as does her response to Savage's project: "Ooh, academia! The eternal pursuit of knowledge" (*Buz'Gem* 25). In fact, we could read Colleen, the gullible professor of Aboriginal literature in Taylor's *alterNatives, a*s a grown-up version of Summer.

What then can we, as scholars, learn from Drew Hayden Taylor's depiction of Summer, the spiritual tourist/scholar? I suspect that we can learn more from what she does not do than from what she does. She reveals very little of herself, even in response to Marianne's probing: "So what is it about

Indians that you find so interesting?" (*Buz'Gem* 66). With this question, Marianne echoes the advice that, as Gregory Sarris recounts, a Pomo-Miwok elder gave to a young woman like Summer at a conference: "Listen ... do you know who you are? Why are you interested? Ask yourself that" (74). We never do know who Summer is. But each of us who work in Aboriginal studies need to ask ourselves that question and be willing to share the answer. And, also unlike Summer, we need to be willing to "taste" cultures unlike our own, to truly enjoy them (or not enjoy them), not just to think about them. After all, as Taylor asserts in the Foreword to *Buz'Gem Blues:* "There is no unique way for a Native person to boil an egg, nor is there a particularly distinctive manner for a Native woman to love her child, and while I may say that we do have a special sense of humour, it is one that is easily appreciated and accepted by all. A Kraft Dinner joke is a Kraft Dinner joke in any culture" (8).

NOTES

1 The British Columbia Aboriginal Tourism Association uses a similar slogan – "Welcoming visitors for centuries" – reminding us that Aboriginal people do participate in the marketing of spiritual tourism.
2 See, for instance, Richard Wagamese's *Keeper'n Me,* Thomas King's *Green Grass, Running Water,* Marie Annharte Baker's "Coyote Columbus Café," and Eden Robinson's "Queen of the North."

3. Taylor has also explored the spiritual tourism issue in his play *alterNatives,* where he examines the ways in which white scholars can also be guilty of a form of spiritual tourism and the ways in which Aboriginal people can be complicit in creating inaccurate academic work.

4. My thanks to Tasha Hubbard for bringing this photograph to my attention.

5. Taylor is one of many Aboriginal writers who have used this kind of parody. For example, Monica Marx and the Red Roots Collective played with spiritual stereotypes in *Those Damn Squaws:* "Dial now. 1-800-I want to be an Indian. You too could be spiritual-fulfilled, just as I was . . . Can I just get your Visa number?" (qtd in Brown)

6. Niels Braroe investigated a real-life situation where Aboriginal people were using strategies of concealment and irony to deal with white demands, and the results of his study reflect the results in Taylor's plays. Braroe studied the interaction of the Cree from the "Short Grass" Reserve and the whites in a nearby village. He found that the Cree often performed in stereotyped roles in order to get what they wanted from the white settlers. One Cree informant said that, when charged with a crime, "[t]he way to get off easy is to act like a dumb Indian in front of the magistrate" (qtd. in Braroe 169). In such interactions, the Cree viewed themselves as "artful and successful exploiters of whitemen" (168). Meanwhile, they often concealed their religion, culture, and even their real (Cree) names from white people, thus hiding a significant part of their identity (130). Presenting a stereotyped mask allowed the Short Grass Cree to maintain their identity out of the judgmental view of the settlers. However, Braroe's interviews with the whites living near the Shortgrass Reserve showed that they viewed the Native people as cultureless, foolish, and irresponsible. In the same way, in *The Baby Blues,* the men's parodic approach allows Summer's different, though equally inaccurate, beliefs to continue.

7 For an excellent critique of research from an Indigenous perspective, see Linda Smith's *Post-Colonial Methodologies*.

Works Cited

Baker, Marie Annharte. "Coyote Columbus Café." *An Anthology of Canadian Native Literature in English*. 2nd ed. Ed. Daniel David Moses and Terry Goldie. Oxford: Oxford University Press, 1998. 191-195.

Basso, Keith. Portraits of the "Whiteman": *Linguistic Play and Cultural Symbols among the Western Apache*. New York: Cambridge University Press, 1979.

Braroe, Niels Winther. *Indian and White: Self Image and Interaction in a Canadian Plains Community*. Stanford, Calif.: Stanford University Press, 1975.

Crosby, Marcia. "Construction of the Imaginary Indian." *By, For and About: Feminist Cultural Politics*. Ed. Wendy Waring. Toronto: Women's Press, 1994. 85113.

Curtis, Edward S. "Hesquiat Maiden and notes." "Index to Portfolio Images–Portfolio 1 to Portfolio 20, Vol. 11." *The Curtis Collection*. http://www.curtis-collection.com/tribe%20data/portfolio%20index/portfolio11.html.

Hoy, Helen. *How Should I Read These?: Native Women Writers in Canada*. Toronto: University of Toronto Press, 2000.

King, Thomas. *Green Grass, Running Water*. Toronto: HarperPerennial, 1999.

Makepeace, Anne. "Dressing Up: Whose Idea Was it Anyway?" American Masters Webpage. http://www.thirteen.org/americanmasters/curtis/dress_about.html

——. "Shooting the Sacred." American Masters Webpage. http://www.thirteen.org/americanmasters/curtis/sacred_about.html

Marx, Monica and the Red Roots Collective. *Those Damn Squaws*. Unpublished.

Nunn, Robert. "Hybridity and Mimicry in the Plays of Drew Hayden Taylor." *Essays on Canadian Writing* (Fall 1998): 95-119.

"Only in God's Country could you meet such interesting souls." *The New York Times Magazine*, part 2 (May 17, 1992): 2-3.

Robinson, Eden. "Queen of the North." *Traplines*. New York: Metropolitan Books, 1996.

Ryan, Allan. *The Trickster Shift: Humour and Irony in Contemporary Native Art*. Vancouver: University of British Columbia Press, 1999.

Sarris, Gregory. *Keeping Slug Woman Alive : A Holistic Approach to American Indian Texts*. Berkeley: University of California Press, 1993.

Taylor, Drew Hayden. *alterNatives*. Vancouver: Talonbooks, 2000.

——. *The Baby Blues*. Vancouver: Talonbooks, 1999.

——. *Buz'Gem Blues*. Vancouver: Talonbooks, 2002.

Thompson, David. "From *Narrative of the Explorations in Western North America, 1784-1812*." *A New Anthology of Canadian Literature in English*. Ed. Donna Bennett and Russell Brown. Toronto: Oxford University Press, 2002. 38-49.

Wagamese, Richard. *Keeper'n Me*. Toronto: Doubleday, 1994.

Your Hand Weighs Exactly One Pound

Misrecognition and "Indian Humour" in Drew Hayden Taylor's Blue-eyed Ojibway *Series*

Rob Appleford

> There was a white trader who had a bad reputation. He was known for his temper and liked to cheat the [Abenaki] Indians who came to trade with him. When they brought in their skins, he would pay for them by the pound, using an old-fashioned balance scale. However, instead of using a counterweight, he would place his hand in the tray and say, "My hand weighs just one pound" (Bruchac 24).

For not the first time in my career, I am feeling a reluctant empathy with Professor David Coward, emeritus lecturer of the University of Leeds French Department. Professor Coward was the champion three years running of the "Boring Lecturer of the Year" contest, held annually at Leeds. Competitors nominated themselves and could speak on any subject. Professor Coward's final triumph in 1976 consisted of an extended Marxist explication of a joke about coconuts. "It wasn't a terribly good joke," he confessed, "but after I had explained it for twenty minutes people began to see its latent merits." He retired from the competition undefeated. In choosing to write a serious paper on funny business, I can only feel envy for Professor Coward's chutzpah (or even for the moxie of his closest rival, a member of the medical faculty, whose lecture on "How to tell right from left" was illustrated by slides of a billiard ball viewed from different angles [Pile 21]). My empathy and envy reflect my reluctance to discuss the politics of what has been called "Indian humour" as it is employed in Drew Hayden Taylor's *Blue-Eyed Ojibway* series, four collections of non-fiction. While many have written serious papers on funny business, there is frequently an uneasy tension in this work between the critical arguments developed to explain or complicate the processes of humour and the jokes used to illustrate these arguments. The unfunny apparatus supplied, the critic dives as quickly as possible into the joke-pool, almost as if she or he is acutely conscious of the killjoy dryness of the task and therefore retells the jokes with a sense of compensatory relief (for the reader as much as for the critic). Freud, in his landmark study *The Joke and its Relation to the Unconscious,* writes that "every joke demands its own audience" (147), and his own discussion displays this capitulation in his discussion of Jewish humour, with joke after joke about stingy fathers and hapless matchmakers. The joke's "demand" seems to seduce the critic into retelling the jokes to the reader and thus participating in the economy of humour from the perspective of the knowing joker rather than that of the unknowing listener. But I will attempt here to resist this demand to surrogate the joker's role and instead focus on the role of the listener, in this case the non-Aboriginal listener, in the economy of "Indian humour." By laughing at Taylor's "Indian humour," the non-Aboriginal listener gains a peculiar purchase within this economy of Aboriginal discourse, a purchase that is not without a charge in the exchange. Instead of belabouring the "latent merits" of "not a terribly good joke" as Professor Coward did in his triumphant lecture, or explicating Taylor's journalism as unreflexive "Indian humour," I will discuss how Taylor's "Indian humour" can be seen to move in two directions, producing and being produced by unstable notions of Aboriginal identity. In my examination of the political misrecognition inherent in "Indian humour," I hope to entertain the aptness of Freud's open remark that *"we do not in the strict sense know what we are laughing at"* (emphasis in original 99).

> WENDY: There was this joke going around at the cop shop: how do you wink at an Indian?
> EILEEN: How?
> Wendy makes like she's shooting a gun. (Mosionier)

It is a given to suggest that a dominant trope in discussions of contemporary Aboriginal discourse is humour, as both a healing mode of recuperation and a satirical mode of resistance. My argument is predicated on exposing a number of misrecognitions in the widespread discussions of "Indian humour," not the least of which involves the conflation of pre-contact uses of humour in Aboriginal communities with its deployment in postcontact discourses. Vine Deloria Jr., in an oft-quoted passage, affirms the centrality of humour in pre-contact Aboriginal communities, especially the mode of "teasing" and its function as a moderating influence on individual egos within these communities:

> Rather than embarrass members of the tribe publicly, people used to tease individuals they considered out of step with the consensus of tribal opinion. In this way egos were preserved and disputes within the tribe of a personal nature were to be held to a minimum. Gradually people learned to anticipate teasing and began to tease themselves as a means of showing humility and at the same time advocating a course of action they deeply believed in. [People] would depreciate their feats to show they were not trying to run roughshod over tribal desires. (147)

It is clear from Deloria's description that the necessary boundaries of subjectivity, where individual "egos" are made to conform to pre-existing "tribal desires," are established through teasing. Thus, the identity of "Indian" is predicated at least in part on the humorous interpellation of the self into "tribal opinion."[1] Compare the above description with the following:

> There is continual laughter, and jests flying all around the wigwam from the time they wake in the morning till the last one goes to sleep. As long as they have anything to eat, and no one is very sick, they are as cheerful and happy as can be. The laughter and droll remarks pass from one to the other, a continual fusillade all around. The old woman says something funny; the children take it up, and laugh at it; all the others repeat it, each with some embellishment, or adding some ludicrous feature, and thus there is continual merriment all day and all evening long. (Gilfallan 64)

This observation was made not by an Aboriginal participant, but by a non-Aboriginal anthropologist studying Anishnaabe (Ojibway) communities in 1901. What is different here is the corollary of this observation given its political context. The emotional health humour is seen to foster here, a humour almost irrepressible, is lent context by the disavowed threat to physical health and well-being signalled in the anthropologist's language. The community is described as a fun bunch, but the anthropologist's caveat that the hilarity ensues "as long as they have *anything* to eat, and no one is *very* sick" (my emphasis) cannot help but evoke the precarious situation of this community in the late nineteenth century, when the "fusillade" of laughter might well be silenced by another, more mortal fusillade. That humour allows the community to be "as cheerful and happy as can be" both reifies the role of humour as a "natural" state of Aboriginal peoples and legitimizes the limits placed on their happiness by colonial control: they are as happy as can be. In this way, "Indian humour" is seen, in one case, to reflect pre-contact humility inside communities, but in the other, postcontact acceptance of externally imposed limits.

> Boozho Dude: Hey, I'm talking to you, *Bozo Dude*.
> (Annharte 192)

What becomes key here is the role of the non-Aboriginal observer in "Indian humour." Humour is by its nature inclusive and pleasurable, as Freud characterizes its "demand." In a homey sense, when someone we like or want to like tells a joke, we enjoy laughing at the joke. But Freud also continues his description by saying that "laughing at the same jokes is evidence of far-reaching psychical compatibility" (147), and here we can begin to see the attraction for the non-Aboriginal participant in the exchange of laughter. By laughing at the same jokes as Aboriginal listeners are perceived to do, non-Aboriginal listeners become temporarily part of the community constructed and implied by this laughter.[2] Delaware writer Daniel David Moses echoes Deloria's conception of "Indian humour" as interpellation, but extends it to include non-Aboriginal participants:

> The first few times I take new friends home to the reserve I have to prepare them, because a large part of how we function is [through] teasing each other. If they're not prepared they're going to feel under attack. The function of teasing, it seems to me, is to help characterize you as an individual. It points out maybe a weakness or maybe just something that's interesting about you. To me, it means they've recognized who you are. A lot of people from mainstream society aren't used to being attacked. It takes a bit of moving around in their head to figure out what's going on, to be comfortable with it. It can be very funny but it's meant as a gesture of recognition. (Ryan 89)

In Moses' description, we can see how the interpellation of the "mainstream" individual through teasing in Aboriginal communities is also an ideological interpellation in the sense that Althusser argues, where "the rituals of ideological recognition [. . .] guarantee for us that we are indeed concrete, individual, distinguishable and (naturally) irreplaceable subjects" (117). In one sense, to be "hailed" (as Althusser calls it) in a "gesture of recognition" (as Moses calls it) allows the non-Aboriginal observer to deny her ideological character at least conditionally, as Althusser affirms (118). Teasing, for Deloria and Moses both, recognizes something unique about the individual, usually something that evokes a subjective life beyond ideology. But this overlooking of ideological position can be only token; the non-Aboriginal teased knows that his recognition by the Aboriginal teasers must either be based on the conscious ignoring of his ideological position, or more importantly, on the acceptance of his ideological position as being "okay," "not a problem," etc. and not a barrier to being accepted as an individual. And in this way, the tease promises a kind of forgiveness, a temporary release from ideological culpability. We may or may not be aware of this contingency when we laugh along with the joke, and thus enjoy its offered pleasure.

There is a danger when this contingent release through teasing is misrecognized as an unproblematic interpellation. An example of this occurs in Clifford Geertz's introduction to his famous essay "Deep Play: Notes on the Balinese Cockfight" (1973). In the essay, Geertz evinces a "thick" anthropological approach to studying culture, but there is an interesting blind spot in the introduction, where, as Kalpana Seshadri-Crooks points out, "the barely acknowledged fact of Geertz's whiteness subtends the entire narrative" (375). After he and his wife join the Balinese villagers in fleeing from police when an illegal cockfight is broken up, Geertz luxuriates in the mockery he and his wife are subjected to by the villagers the next morning: "they gleefully mimicked [...] our graceless style of running and what they claimed were our panic-stricken facial expressions" (416). Geertz sees this teasing by "our co-villagers," coupled with his refusal to "pull out our papers" for the police instead of fleeing, as evidence that he had penetrated the veil of Balinese culture and had been accepted as part of the community. However, Seshadri-Crooks introduces the equally compelling explanation that "the entire possibility of comedy here [. . .] derives from Geertz's and his wife's whiteness." She argues that Geertz's refusal to perform privilege when confronted by the authorities – choosing to flee rather than show the cops his papers – does not efface his "Distinguished Visitor status" (Geertz 416) but instead renders his performed loss of agency even more laughable in the eyes of the Balinese villagers, who had no choice but to flee: "the loss [of Geertz's agency] inheres in the dominant subject's limited and inconsequential decision *not* to perform [the norm of white privilege], a decision to which the conceit of whiteness lends a solemn gravity" (374-5). Sometimes, it is awfully tempting to think that laughing *at* is synonymous with laughing with, and ignore the interpellative work that must be done to move between the two prepositions.[3]

While there is the attraction of forgetting one's ideological position, if only for a moment, in the enjoyment of the laughter, there is also the attraction of being able to discursively renovate this position through this enjoyment. In his discussion of comic world view in Anishnaabe culture and religion, Lawrence W. Gross (Anishnaabe) affirms that there are two persistent themes in his people's myths, "a second chance" and "forgiveness," and he ties these motifs together in his explanation of Anishnaabe ethical generosity: "in allowing for human error the myths encourage self-forgiveness and giving oneself a second chance" (446). Thus, "human error" allows us all to self-forgive, and for the non-Aboriginal participant, to selectively renovate our only partially denied ideological character through the inclusive activity of laughter. As Kenneth Lincoln puts it in his discussion of "Indi'n Humor," interracial teasing "targets issues with an attention that roughs its audience affectionately, Indian-to-white" (26). "Indian humour," as it has been described, seems to offer such a promise, where non-Aboriginal listeners can vicariously enjoy an insider's glimpse of culture while at the same time refigure how they see themselves as an "affectionately roughed" audience. The tendency here, when being teased by an indigenous joker, is for the non-indigenous victim to renovate his own subjectivity and misrecognize the shared laughter as unproblematically concerted. But we can begin to see the infinite regress triggered by the joking relationship: we are made the butt of the joker's joke; the joker laughs at our self-conscious discomfort; we laugh with good humour at being the butt of the joke; the joker laughs at our laughter; we laugh at being laughed at a second time; the joker laughs at our pretension that we have lost our outsider status through being laughed at; we laugh at the joker's third fusillade of laughter and feel part of the joker's audience; and so it goes. The punch in the punch line seems to be endlessly deferred.

At the start of this essay, I suggested that "Indian humour" operates as an economic system of exchange, and this idea of willful misrecognition I have foregrounded is closely tied to the misrecognition of symbolic and cultural practices within an economic system. Pierre Bourdieu's work on forms of capital has shown us that the value of objects and practices in an economic system is predicated on the relative effort needed to convert these objects and practices into "real money." As Bourdieu points out, the conversion of symbolic and cultural capital into economic capital must be enacted at the same time that it is denied: "As everyone knows, priceless things have their price, and the extreme difficulty of converting certain practices and certain objects into money is only due to the fact that this conversion is refused in the very intention that produces them, which is nothing other than the denial *(Verneinung)* of the economy" (242). The more occluded and stubborn the practice or object is in the process of conversion, the more valuable it becomes. In the context of "Indian humour," the gesture of recognition offered by the Aboriginal tease must be misrecognized as inclusive and uninflected by capital. Yet because the lure of token participation for a non-Aboriginal observer is so strong, and the ideological positioning so entrenched in privilege, the "priceless" laughter in a real sense always has economic conversion as its endgame. We like to laugh, "Indian humour" lets us laugh and be "recognized" with "rough affection," and we will pay to participate. We do so through direct purchase of products by Aboriginal humourists, or, flexing our institutional muscles, through the publication of articles promoting these humourists, the selection of their work for course syllabi, and the fostering of discourse which makes the attraction of "Indian humour" (and those who do it) commonplace, naturalized, and ubiquitous.

> The [AIM] movement had its humorous moments. The Indians of Milwaukee spread the rumour that they were going to invade the Milwaukee Yacht Club so they could have "Red Sons in the Sail Set," but it was rumour, nothing more. (Deloria 149)

In case you thought that I could defer his entrance indefinitely, enter Drew Hayden Taylor, speaker's fee in hand. Taylor's version of "Indian humour" can be refreshingly candid on this issue of misrecognition. He constantly reminds his non-Aboriginal audience of the economic utility of his humour as a career move, and his jokes' effect relies in large measure on our knowing complicity in this economy:

> I'm fairly certain I'm not the fiery radical type [. . .] I find radicals don't get paid nearly enough. (1998: 85)

> Take from my suggestions what you will. I'm getting paid regardless. (1999: 25)

> Hopefully, there's stuff here that will tickle your funnybone, make you sad, make you angry, and perhaps make you think "I spent almost $20 on this!" (2004: 8)

> I acknowledge that these same people [who ask repetitive questions] may buy my books [. . .] and often it's their tax money that is indirectly being rerouted into my wallet via reading fees. (2004: 138)

While his teasing is often "rough affection," it also forces us to acknowledge that this affection is predicated on a denial of our ideological positioning. His playful warning to not "be surprised if all us Indians are booted off the reserve and end up in your 'burbs' looking for affordable split-level duplexes" (1998: 88) is also a caution about denying the material realities of Aboriginal peoples, and how our ensconced privilege is the product of an ongoing colonial legacy. Taylor continually pushes the envelope of complicity between audience and joker, interleaving "affectionate roughing" and recognition with harsher treatment, as with his take on Residential schooling of Aboriginal children: "and as we all know, the conjugation of [French] verbs is best taught through anal penetration. Maybe that's why I failed French in Grade 11" (2002: 19).

Yet despite his understanding of the misrecognition inherent in the joking relationship, and his flagging of this misrecognition in his journalism, Taylor is also paradoxically committed to using humour as a more "healing" and less antagonistic mode of communication between non-Aboriginals and Aboriginals, where the misrecognition of position must be tacitly denied. "Humour should amuse, not abuse," he affirms (2002: 49), and he frequently expresses frustration at non-Aboriginals who don't just want to enjoy the joke as pleasurable release. When trying to understand the stiff reaction to one of his plays when it was performed for a Port Dover summer-theatre audience, Taylor laments that "perhaps, in some way, they wanted to [be made to] feel guilty by what they saw, to be kicked in the ribs by social tragedy their ancestors had caused rather than give in to the healing powers of humour" (2002: 92). While consistency is anathema to any humourist, and a humourist can't be expected to check his funnybone for osseous homogeneity before he cracks a joke, I do find it necessary to consider possible reasons why Taylor's use of humour both abuses and amuses, sometimes simultaneously.

One possibility lies in the ambiguous relationship Taylor recognizes in his status as "Native informant." Part of the allure of "Indian humour" for the non-Aboriginal participant, as I have argued, lies in the temporary interpellation the joking relationship permits. And it is important to point out that such interpellation is influenced by our assumption that the joker is a legitimate member in good standing with his Aboriginal community. If we can feel incorporated into a community through laughter, we must trust that the joker can interpellate us based upon his knowing status as a cultural insider. This is especially vital if the joker pokes fun at his own people, as Taylor frequently does. If this were not so, to laugh at Taylor's jokes about the Aboriginal fascination with golf or sourpussed Aboriginal politicians would leave the non-Aboriginal participant distinctly uncomfortable, akin to enjoying a chuckle with a non-Jewish person telling jokes about Jews.

Taylor himself has exhibited an interesting shift in his own understanding of himself as a "Native informant." In his second collection of essays, he proudly tells us that

> One Native teacher at a college told me at the launch [of his first collection of essays] that she had been putting together a course description on Native Criticism and

was worried because she didn't have a textbook. Until now. (1999: i)

This claim is supported by many non-Aboriginal scholars and teachers who make use of Taylor's non-fiction in their examinations of Aboriginal worldviews. For example, Roger Spielmann writes:

> I often use the writings of Drew Hayden Taylor to begin my [Native Studies] classes; they are usually thought-provoking and there is a kind of biting humour to them. Sometimes non-Native students approach me after class and tell me that they are offended by a particular reading. I usually invite them to try and take off their own cultural glasses and, at least for a moment, put on Anishnaabe glasses and try to grasp a fleeting glimpse of the world through the Anishnaabe perspective. (111)

Such a conflation of an individual's point of view with that of an entire people's can only be achieved if that individual is taken to be a comfortable metonym of his people, a communal mouthpiece rather than an idiosyncratic mouthypiece. Taylor's pride in being a self-described "basic grass-roots person of Indigenous descent" (2002: 51) who is taken up as a de facto authority on "Native Criticism" is alloyed somewhat in his last collection of essays. He laments that his unfamiliarity with Anishnaabe, his people's language, forces him to write "as best as I can" about Aboriginal experiences from a "filtered perspective"

(2004: 11). This humility suggests Taylor's deepening wisdom about his role as a spokesperson for the "Aboriginal perspective," and given the political volatility of self-definition in Aboriginal circles, it is also a wisdom born under punches.

> One day, the [Abenaki] Indians had had enough. They purchased a set of weights and went to the man's store to confront him as a cheat. The white trader, though, became angry, pulled out his gun and shot at them. The Indians shot back and killed the man. (Bruchac 24)

While Taylor styles himself as an Aboriginal humourist, he is also careful to point out that he is "the product of a White father I never knew, and an Ojibway woman who evidently couldn't run fast enough" (1998: 3). As a mixed-blood person who is Anishnaabe-identified (he spent his first eighteen years on his Curve Lake reserve), Taylor sees himself as occupying a usefully liminal space between non-Aboriginal and Aboriginal cultures. As indicated by the non-fiction collections' running subtitle – "Funny, You Don't Look Like One" – Taylor plays upon his potential to "make a great undercover agent for one of the Native political organizations" because of his non-Aboriginal appearance:

> One time a friend and I were coming out of a rather upscale bar [...] and managed to catch a cab. We thanked the cab driver for being so comfortably close on such a

cold night. He shrugged and nonchalantly talked about knowing what bars to drive around. "If you're not careful, all you get is drunk Indians." I hiccuped. (1998: 5)

In an effective way, this anecdote prevents the non-Aboriginal reader from comfortably interpreting the behaviour of Taylor within the episode. On one hand, we can assume that his "hiccup" was an intentional joke meant to illustrate the glitches in the cab driver's "Indian radar," a signal of controlled mockery. But on the other hand, Taylor leaves suspended the idea that he was a "drunk Indian" at that moment, and that his hiccup was in fact an inadvertent challenge to the cab driver's assumption that Indians don't have as much right to be drunk as anyone else. Misrecognition occurs within the moment of the episode itself and within the moment when the story is interpreted by the reader; both moments are shown to be problematic because they involve intentional and cultural assumptions about the author that are rehearsed without being corrected outright by Taylor. This suspension of interpretation is an effective ironic strategy that allows the humourist to slip between the position of subject (the sly hiccuper) and object (the "drunk Indian") without lending either position primacy. Lois Leeven, in her examination of ethnic humour, suggests that it is this mobility on the part of the ethnic joker that makes visible the distinctions often elided in cross-cultural discourse, distinctions between

> the individual self and the collective (i.e., ethnic) identity; between the assimilated self and the ethnic self; and between the self as object and the self as subject – a situation that arises whenever an ethnic speaking subject tells a joke of which, in terms of ethnicity, s/he is also an object. (41)

In this way, Taylor mounts an effective defence against those non-Aboriginal readers who seek to conflate the act of laughing with the act of secure definition.

What is perhaps a touchier issue here is not Taylor's evasive manoeuver in the service of ethnic freeplay, but rather how Aboriginal commentators have reacted to such freeplay in light of expectations about the ideological function of Aboriginal identity. Several Native American scholars such as Elizabeth Cook-Lynn (Crow Creek Sioux) decry the absence of what she calls an "inner-unfolding theory of Native culture" in the intellectual and cultural resurgence of indigenous peoples in the last century (70). For Cook-Lynn, any attempt to evolve an effective political strategy which can challenge hegemony must be mounted from within recognizably traditional Aboriginal intellectual and communal boundaries. There is an important folding-over in Cook-Lynn's definition of cultural authenticity and efficacy. She voices concern over three discrete developments: the lack of indigenous community-based intellectual work, the prominence of "mixed-blood" writers and critics, and the popularity of humour in contemporary Aboriginal expression. It is clear that Cook-Lynn attributes a distinct cause and effect relationship in their development. She suggests that it is less likely that mixed-blood Aboriginal writers will continue to remain (or have ever lived) within Aboriginal communities, and that they will gravitate to urban centres more readily to pursue their careers:

> the mixed-blood literary phenomena is not generated from the inside of tribal culture since many of the practitioners admit they have been removed from cultural influence through urbanization [...] Separation of these writers from indigenous communities (reservation or urban) indicates that this is a literary movement of disengagement. (70)

This distinction between mixed-blood writers living in urban spaces and full-blood writers who participate in the day-to-day life of the community, she suggests through implication, leads the former to employ comedic means whereby they can both earn a living in dominant culture and ameliorate their feeling of "disengagement" from traditional culture: "are our [writers] just people who glibly use the English language to entertain us, to keep us amused and preoccupied so that we are no longer capable of making the distinction between the poet and the stand-up comedian?" (74). Cook-Lynn's distrust of humour here is a distrust of its role as cultural capital, whereby "Indian humour" helps in the inexorable erosion of indigenous communities and the values they need to maintain to survive.

It is apparent that in this depiction of humour's co-opted role, there is an implied political shape to the Aboriginal subject's ethnic expression, a teleology either implicit or explicit. Kathryn W. Shanley (Assiniboine/Nakota) emphasizes the inherently political nature of Native American identity, an identity which she argues must frame itself in relation to Aboriginal peoples and their political struggles and by extension make political demands on its readers:

> An Indian can write about a teapot or a blue balloon or a day at the Field Museum of Natural History, but he or she must situate himself or herself in relation to Indian people. Does that mean that, of necessity, being an American Indian writer means being political? In my opinion, the answer is yes, because a claim to Indian cultural roots places the individual in a political position (whether or not the person making such a declaration recognizes it as such). (696)

While this debate is mainly situated in the specifically American context of colonialism and the development of Critical Race theory in the academy, two entwined discourses distinct in many ways from the trajectory of Canadian colonial call-response, the issue is also plainly a vexing one for Taylor. The humourist expresses irritation over being misrecognized as the "wrong" ethnicity by both Aboriginal and non-Aboriginal peoples, and he famously coins himself a "Special Occasion": the founder of a half Ojibway, half Caucasian nation (1998: 8). This is a joke, of course. Taylor consistently grounds his humour in his Anishnaabe heritage, and his writing playfully experiments with the expectations this heritage evokes. But the physical misrecognition as neither/nor is coupled with an anxiety over the ideological misrecognition of what his heritage can allow him to express. Taylor, who calls himself not only an urban Indian but an "Urbane Indian" (1998: 102) has been taken to task by several within the Aboriginal community, not only for his controversial opinions, but for his unexamined right to articulate them as an Aboriginal spokesperson. As with his candid exposure of the economic aspects of "Indian Humour," Taylor refuses to skirt over the instances of discontent he has caused. From a dismissive reaction from an Aboriginal politician who "criticized me for not spending more time writing about important issues that were more pertinent to our people" (2002: 35), to a "bizarre growing attitude of resentment" from some Aboriginal people towards his supposedly flippant examination of identity issues (103), Taylor documents with obvious anger, perplexity and some relish his effect on Aboriginal readers who resent his writing. This dissension culminates in an extended discussion of Taylor's place with the Anishnaabe community in the final collection, where he squares off with an Anishnaabe "friend" who severely reprimands him for pursuing a documentary project involving Aboriginal erotica, a category the friend refuses to recognize. In this essay, Taylor "learns" that there are two kinds of Anishnaabe people: the *regular* Anishnaabe and the "*with-it* Aboriginals" (original emphasis). According to his nameless upbraider, *regular* Anishnaabe refuse to participate in the mainstream values and desires of non-Aboriginal audiences and know when things are truly traditional, whereas *with-its* are "Aboriginal artists doing what they do because they have been corrupted by dominant society" (2004: 68). Despite Taylor's point that other reserve-based Anishnaabe artists like Kateri Akiwenzie-Damm were also interested in collecting and writing Aboriginal erotica, his "friend" refused to allow that *regulars* and *with-its* were impossible categories to maintain. Taylor ends the essay with a sarcastic sigh, "Oh well. What do I know?," and a reluctant acceptance of the *with-it* label (70).

As an outside observer, it is tempting to dismiss such cavilling as a biassed response to a successful Aboriginal writer, the product of blinkered thinking easily dismissed. However, when this criticism is not considered as a truth claim but as a boundary marker which calls into question the unreflexive acceptance – by non-Aboriginal scholars, critics and readers – of an individual artist as a metonym for Aboriginal community, we can see how Taylor's use of humour is not simply a one-way communication, an affectionate roughing from Indian to white. Just as teasing in a pre-contact Aboriginal context involves the reminder to the individual not to "run roughshod over tribal desires" (Deloria, 147), the castigation of Taylor by some members of the Aboriginal community suggests another reminder. However, in this post-contact and postcolonial moment, the caution involves not the enforcement of the limits of self-interest within the tribe, but rather the boundary past which one is *not* only not considered a member of the tribe, but *not* considered a legitimate product of the tribe's value system.

At stake here in Taylor's "Indian humour" is the mutually constitutive relationship between the two terms, how this humour not only interpellates non-Aboriginal participants, but also interpellates the Aboriginal person who is himself recognized in a gesture of recognition through the expression of this humour. "Indian humour" functions in this context as a ma(r)ker of authentic Aboriginal identity, whereby the joker can constitute himself as simultaneously *regular* and *with-it*. We can see this two-way process at play in the work of other Aboriginal writers such as Sherman Alexie (Spokane/Cœur d'Alene), who valorize less the interpellative function of "Indian humour" across cultures (as Taylor does) than its function as a cultural gate-keeper: "I load my books with stuff, just load 'em up. I call them 'Indian trapdoors.' You know, Indians fall in, white people just walk right over them [...] I really want the subtext for Indians" (Purdy 15). It is easy to see this gate-keeping as a necessary and vital way to preserve cultural autonomy. But we can also consider Alexie's own complex relationship to his Spokane/Cœur d'Alene community. Like many Aboriginal writers, Alexie endures a persistent level of distrust within his own community, not only for the transgressive content of his writing but for his right to write this content. In an interview with Erik Himmelsbach, Alexie discusses this distrust quite candidly:

> While Alexie has enlightened the world at large about the contemporary American Indian experience, his tribe has essentially shunned him. Back at the Spokane Reservation in Wellpinit, Wash., people have strong, often unfavorable opinions about the author who, as a child, often whiled away his days alone in his room playing Dungeons & Dragons or Nerf basketball. "I was a divisive presence

on the reservation when I was 7," he recalls. "I was a weird, eccentric, very arrogant little boy. The writing doesn't change anybody's opinion of me. If anything, it's intensified it."

We can recognize how the "Indian trapdoors" not only let Indians in, but reify Alexie's own status as a trapdoor-maker, one whose Aboriginal identity is at least in part constituted by the gesture of recognition by Aboriginal readers that they "get it" and by extension "get him" as a *regular* Aboriginal person despite his *with-it* predilections.

When the necessary distinctions are recognized in the functions of "Indian humour," as traditional interpellation, as cultural gate-keeping, and as mutual constitution, we can begin to see how defining this humour in practice becomes highly complicated. For instance, in his pioneering study of Cache Creek Pomo discourse *Keeping Slug Woman Alive: A Holistic Approach to American Indian Texts,* Greg Sarris relates many humorous instances where Mabel Mckay, a noted Pomo healer, uses jokes to remind her interlocutors of their own preconceptions about Native American identity: " 'What do you do for poison oak?' a student once asked in a large auditorium where Mabel was being interviewed as a native healer. 'Calamine lotion,' Mabel answered" (17). Sarris underlines the doubled effect of her dry answer, whereby Mckay "acknowledged that she is an Indian but, at the same time, introduced the fact that she is a contemporary American, which redefined the student's notion of 'Indian'" (18). This doubled effect of redefinition as Indian/American rests upon Mckay's secure identity as a Cache Creek Pomo woman who can control (and complicate) how she is perceived by non-Aboriginals; there is little anxiety over the relationship between *regular* and *with-it* status. She is neither and both. Yet, when Alexie and Taylor echo this discursive maneuver, there are pronounced elements of frustration and anxiety in their bait-and-switch:

> "Sherman," asks the critic, "how does your work apply to the oral tradition?"
>
> "Well," I say, as I hold my latest book close to me, "it doesn't apply at all because I type this. And I'm really, really quiet when I'm typing it." (Alexie 6)
>
> Question two: "When you write your plays or stories, do you write for a specifically Native audience or a White audience?" My answer: "I'm usually alone in my room when I write, except for my dying cactus. So I guess that means I write for my dying cactus." (Taylor 1998: 67)
>
> We get up in the morning, put our clothes on, have coffee (usually fully or extra-caffinated [sic]), go to the bathroom . . . Yes, Indians do go to the bathroom but in a secret Indian way that can't be revealed. (Taylor 1998: 108)

> Passing judgement on other people isn't a particularly Aboriginal thing to do. I know this because an eagle came to me in my dreams, along with a coyote and a raven; they landed on the tree of peace, smoked a peace pipe, ate a baloney sandwich, played some bingo, and then told me so. (1999: 107)

The evasion in these sarcastic rejoinders is less about multivalence (as with Mackay) than about frustration with the expectations of non-Aboriginal audiences and readers who have specific reductive expectations about Aboriginal identity. And this frustration can be seen to be profound, since what is at stake is the kind of subject non-Aboriginal observers will allow Taylor and Alexie to be, if for no other reason than that the economic incentive to patronize Aboriginal writers in the cultural marketplace is predicated as much on perceived authenticity of the voice as on what that voice is saying. While there is a market for what Cook-Lynn derisively calls "Indians who think they can rise to the challenge of life on the entertainment pages," the price of this stock is volatile. The affectionate roughing has clearly just gotten a little rougher.

> We have to be careful to not only present representations of Indian people that are palatable to the mainstream audience, or else we risk losing our authenticity. If we only offer certain types, if we agree to offer only that which is palatable, we are in danger of making invisible all

> those others. [...] Not all Indians are funny, either. Some of us are mad. (Nolan 80)

> [...] Then, just out of curiosity, [the Abenaki Indians] cut his hand off and put it on the scale, using their weights. They felt really bad when they discovered his hand weighed exactly one pound. (Bruchac 24)

What everyone wouldn't give for a simple joke about coconuts right about now.

While I do feel I may have bested Professor Coward, I must still reiterate my intentions for this essay. I did not feel the need to explicate the "latent merits" of Taylor's "Indian humour"; his jokes stand on their own merits, and will continue to amuse or abuse according to the reader's expectations and sensibility. What I have attempted to do is point out the misrecognitions inherent in an unreflexive acceptance of "Indian humour" as natural, straightforward and unproblematic as an interpretative trope. The rolling epigraph to this essay, describing the unfortunate business dealings of the white trader and his Abenaki clients, can be mobilized as a fitting summary. We, as non-Aboriginal listeners, can laugh unproblematically at the irony of the dishonest trader's hand actually weighing one pound. We can enjoy a slightly more nasty laugh at the comeuppance he receives from the Abenaki Indians, a laughter we could imagine is shared by Aboriginal listeners whose history would predispose them to enjoy this comeuppance, but only if we divorce ourselves from the ideological position the trader occupies. It's not *our* hand, after all. But the deeper levels of the irony begin to force us to throat our laughter more hollowly. The "dead hand" of colonialism – with its attribution of authority, abrogation of responsibility, its selective interpellation – may be challenged and severed by the Indians, but it still weighs on the exchange of cultural capital between non-Aboriginal and Aboriginal peoples. It is still the standard measurement of exchange value in colonial discourse. It becomes a pressing question whether non-Aboriginal listeners can in fact laugh at this joke in good conscience. Or is our laughter based on a complex nesting of denials? A denial that our own hand weighs just one pound? A denial that we assume the Aboriginal joker's hand also must weigh the same as ours? A denial that he is itching to find out *exactly* how much our hand weighs? A denial that the scales can never be truly fair in this exchange? What a closer inspection of Drew Hayden's "Indian humour" reveals is the fact that such a humour is not the balm for inter-ethnic or inter-cultural tension and ambiguity. The "fusillades" of laughter it inspires are dangerously buckshot. Rather than revealing to us how discontinuities are overcome in the joke's telling, the relationship "Indian humour" creates can be seen as foregrounding what Ralph Ellison calls "an ironic awareness of the joke that always lies between appearance and reality, between the discontinuity of social tradition and that sense of the past which clings to the mind" (61). As non-Aboriginal listeners, we do not in the strict sense know, or perhaps can ever know, what we are laughing at.

NOTES

1 *Interpellation:* Key term in Louis Althusser's theory of ideology: [Althusser] argues that ideology "recruits" individuals and transforms them, through the "ideological recognition function," into subjects. This recognition function is the process of interpellation: ideology "interpellates" or "hails" individuals, that is, addresses itself directly to them. Althusser gives as his example a policeman hailing an individual by calling, "Hey, you there!" The hailed individual will turn around, recognize himself as the one who was hailed, and in the process become constituted as a subject. All hailed individuals, recognizing or misrecognizing themselves in the address, are transformed into subjects conceiving of themselves as free and autonomous members of a society that has in fact constructed them. (King 567)
2 Susan Bennett provides an example of this tendency to authorize non-Aboriginal responses to "Indian humour" through the appeal to Aboriginal responses to such humour in a description of an Alberta Theatre Projects (ATP) production of Tomson Highway's *The Rez Sisters* in 1990:

As a white woman in an almost entirely white audience ... I was particularly unsettled by the performance preface (a convention of ATP productions) which was given to the audience by a white male representing the company. He told us that we should enjoy the play, that it was appropriate to laugh and that Native audiences had been in to see this particular production and had laughed too. (19)

3 In her discussion of minority humour, Doris Sommer writes: "The release [of repressive energy] is a double pleasure for the listener: both the intellectual satisfaction of getting the joke, and the political pleasure of gloating over the second person who doesn't get it . . . the corollary mistake is to imagine that one is the ideal audience, rather than the butt of the joke" (100-101).

Works Cited

Alexie, Sherman. "The Unauthorized Biography of Me." *Here First: Autobiographical Essays by Native American Writers.* Ed. Arnold Krupat and Brian Swann. New York: The Modern Library, 2000: 3-14.

Annharte. "Coyote Columbus Café." *An Anthology of Canadian Native Literature in English.* 2nd ed. Ed. Daniel David Moses and Terry Goldie. Toronto: Oxford University Press, 1998: 191-195.

Bennett, Susan. "Who Speaks?: Representations of Native Women in Some Canadian Plays." *Canadian Journal of Drama and Theatre* 1.2 (1991): 13-25.

Bourdieu, Pierre. "The Forms of Capital." *Handbook of Theory and Research for the Sociology of Education.* Ed. John G. Richardson. New York: Greenwood Press, 1986: 241-260.

Bruchac, Joseph. "Striking the Pole: American Indian Humor." *Parabola* 12.4 (Winter 1987): 22-29.

Cook-Lynn, Elizabeth. "American Indian Intellectualism and the New Indian Story." *American Indian Quarterly* 20.1 (Winter 1996): 57-76.

Deloria, Jr., Vine. *Custer Died For Your Sins: An Indian Manifesto.* New York: Macmillian, 1969.

Ellison, Ralph. "Change the Joke and Slip the Yoke." *Mother Wit from the Laughing Barrel.* Ed. Alan Dundes. Englewood Cliffs: Prentice, 1973: 56-64.

Freud, Sigmund. *The Joke and its Relation to the Unconscious.* 1905. Trans. Joyce Crick. Toronto: Penguin, 2002.

Geertz, Clifford. *The Interpretation of Cultures: Selected Essays.* New York: Basic Books, 1973.

Gilfallan, J.A. "The Ojibways of Minnesota." *Collections of the Minnesota Historical Society* 9 (1901): 55-128.

Gross, Lawrence W. "The Comic Vision of Anishnaabe Culture and Religion." *American Indian Quarterly* 26.3 (Summer 2002): 435-459.

Himmelsbach, Erik. "The Reluctant Spokesman." *Los Angeles Times* (17 December 1996): d1.

King, Ross. "Interpellation." *Encyclopedia of Contemporary Literary Theory: Approaches, Scholars, Terms.* Ed. and comp. Irena K. Makaryk. Toronto: University of Toronto Press, 1993. 566-567.

Leveen, Lois. "Only When I Laugh: Textual Dynamics of Ethnic Humor." *MELUS* 21.4 (Winter 1996): 29-55.

Lincoln, Kenneth. *Indi'n Humor: Bicultural Play in Native America.* New York: Oxford University Press, 1993.

Mosionier, Beatrice. *Night of the Trickster* (unpublished playscript). U of Guelph: Native Earth Archives, 1992. xz1 msa875015

Nolan, Yvette. "Selling Myself: The Value of an Artist." *Zeitschrift Für Kanada-Studien* 19.1 (1999): 74-84.

Pile, Stephen. *The Incomplete Book of Failures.* New York: E.P. Dutton, 1979.

Purdy, John. "Crossroads: An Interview with Sherman Alexie." *Studies in American Indian Literatures* 9.4 (Winter 1997): 1-18.

Ryan, Alan J. *The Trickster Shift: Humour and Irony in Contemporary Native Art.* Vancouver: UBC Press, 1999.

Sarris, Greg. *Keeping Slug Woman Alive: A Holistic Approach to American Indian Texts*. Berkeley: University California Press, 1993.

Seshadri-Crooks, Kalpana. "The Comedy of Domination: Psychoanalysis and the Conceit of Whiteness." *The Psychoanalysis of Race*. Ed. Christopher Lane. New York: Columbia University Press, 1998: 353-379.

Shanley, Kathryn W. "The Indians America Loves to Love and Read: American Indian Identity and Cultural Appropriation." *American Indian Quarterly* 21.4 (Autumn 1997): 675-702.

Sommer, Doris. "Be-longing and Bi-lingual States." *Diacritics* 29.4 (1999): 84-115.

Spielmann, Roger. *You're So Fat!: Exploring Ojibwe Discourse*. Toronto: University Toronto Press, 1998.

Taylor, Drew Hayden. *Futile Observations of a Blue-Eyed Ojibway: Funny, You Don't Look Like One, #4*. Penticton, B.C.: Theytus Books, 2004.

———. *Furious Observations of a Blue-Eyed Ojibway: Funny, You Don't Look Like One Two Three*. Penticton, B.C.: Theytus Books, 2002.

———. *Further Adventures of a Blue-Eyed Ojibway: Funny, You Don't Look Like One Two*. Penticton, B.C.: Theytus Books, 1999.

———. *Funny, You Don't Look Like One: Observations from a Blue-Eyed Ojibway*. Rev. ed. Penticton, B.C.: Theytus Books, 1998.

Introduction to
Girl Who Loved Her Horses

RIC KNOWLES AND MONIQUE MOJICA

[Editor's note: the following is reprinted from *Staging Coyote's Dream: An Anthology of First Nations Drama in English,* where it precedes the full text of *Girl Who Loved Her Horses.*]

[It may help the reader to have a brief plot summary. A young Native man, Ralph, walking down a city street, comes upon what remains of a large chalk drawing of a horse on a brick wall, mostly obscured by posters except for its eyes, which are "terrifying and angry." As the lights go down on Ralph, they come up on the horse on another part of the stage: it dances its rage. The scene shifts to a reserve. William, former Chief of the reserve, owns a marina, built with misappropriated Band funds. It is not doing well. His wife, Shelley, has just quit her daycare job in despair. They are joined by Ralph, Shelley's brother, who tells them about the drawing. They recall the kitchen wall Ralph and Shelley's mother set aside for kids to draw on, the "Everything Wall," and a shy girl, Danielle, who came to the house and covered the wall with an astonishing image of a horse. The play moves back in time to their childhood. The three children are joined by the extremely timorous Danielle, who draws her magnificent horse, the animal emerging from the wall and allowing the girl to bask in its radiant energy. In the weeks to come, she returns to the freshly cleared wall and repeats her drawing. William humiliates her by forcing her to draw a dog, which she does poorly. Ralph has a moment when the horse comes alive for him too and he nearly touches it. Danielle is taken away to the city by her alcoholic mother and her mother's violent boyfriend, and nothing is heard of her from that day to the moment when Ralph sees the remnants of the chalk drawing on the brick wall in the city. Ralph takes Shelley and William to the place, and as they tear the posters away from the wall, the horse takes shape. The picture affects them all deeply. Shelley makes the decision to return to her daycare job, and to refuse to give up on a child who covers sheets of paper with black crayon. They leave the stage, and the play ends with this stage direction:

> From inside the wall on the empty stage, the Horse appears, an angry and frustrated one. Still filled with rage, he dances and raises his arms to the wall, still facing the audience, as if calling forth a power. The wall begins to radiate and pulsate, then the image of the Horse painted on the wall begins to glow, solidify and take shape at his urging. The picture of the horse gets brighter, stronger, and more brilliant until the wall is seething in colour and presence. The magic and power of the Horse has returned.

But unfortunately nobody's there to see it. The lights go down. (*Staging* 359)]

Drew Hayden Taylor is an Ojibway from Ontario's Curve Lake First Nation. In the ten years since he won the Chalmers Canadian Play Award for his first play, *Toronto at Dreamer's Rock,* he has established himself as one of the country's most prolific and most frequently produced playwrights as well as a respected television, film, short story, and essay writer. His plays include a trilogy (*Someday, Only Drunks and Children Tell the Truth,* and *400 Kilometres*); a projected "blues" tetralogy (which so far includes *The Bootlegger Blues, The Baby Blues,* and *The Buz'Gem Blues*); a wicked intercultural satire of, among other things, higher education *(alterNatives);* an adaptation of Bertolt Brecht's Mahagonny *(Sucker Falls)*; four plays for young audiences (*The Boy in the Treehouse, Toronto at Dreamer's Rock* and its sequel, *Toronto@Dreamers Rock.com,* and *Girl Who Loved Her Horses*); and a sort of agit-prop Christmas Carol about funding Native education *(Education is Our Right)*. Most of these are published, remain in print, and are regularly produced across the country. He has also published three popular collections of essays under the title, *Funny, You Don't Look Like One: Observations of a Blue-Eyed Ojibway*, and he has served for a time as Artistic Director of Native Earth Performing Arts.

In his best-known plays Taylor adopts, adapts, and rings variations on the sit-com genre, and the apparent familiarity of the form has gained him access to theatres across the country that are not noted for producing Native work. These plays use a subversive brand of satiric humour to probe some of the most sensitive cultural and intercultural issues of our time. But there is another, more spiritual side to Taylor's dramatic work that is most apparent in his plays for young audiences, including of course *Girl Who Loved Her Horses,* which in the preface to its Talonbooks publication Taylor calls "my personal favourite of everything I have ever written" (6). First produced by Theatre Direct Canada in April 1995 at the Theatre Centre in Toronto under the direction of Richard Greenblatt, Girl is perhaps most readily classifiable as a memory play. The central action is framed by the contemporary stories of three adult characters, Shelley, Ralph, and William, and their memories of events fifteen years earlier, triggered by the appearance, as graffiti on an old brick wall, of the worn but still startling image of a horse, its eyes terrifying, animalistic, and angry. But this play does not function like the memory play of western tradition. It doesn't explain away disturbing or traumatic childhood events, bringing satisfying and therapeutic resolutions to the tensions and conflicts of the past and leaving both the characters and the audience refreshed and ready to return to the quotidian world purged of their discontents. In this play the calm and complacent surface of the everyday life of the past and present, as well as of the audience, is ruptured by the insistent intrusion of the numinous.

Girl Who Loved Her Horses might also be read as a "loss of innocence" narrative about art and identity, a flashback to simpler times when, as to "the traditionally minded Inuit, the purpose in carving was to let free the image or spirit trapped within the stone," and "once the image was free, and the stone carved, they would move on" (322). In this reading, the adult characters remember the "wild and free eyes" of the childhood drawing of the horse almost with nostalgia. They conjure for themselves a time before Ralph started studying to be a cop, before William learned to defraud the band to fund his business, and before Shelley learned to give up on troubled students – a time "way back when," when "Indian names said something about who you were or what you did" (357), and when honouring the spirit of the fish one was about to hunt may have been more than an "old Indian line" used to lure or detour tourists (318). This reading, focusing on a stunning final image that "nobody's there to see" (359) might consider the play to be a lament for an irrecoverably lost time when the world of spirit and that of everyday life were inextricably intertwined.

But the play won't quite sit still for either of these readings. Not only has this playwright, so clever with words and dialogue, daringly placed at the play's centre an almost silent title character, a troubled but magical young girl whom we never see in the present tense of the frame story (and who therefore remains an unknown rupture in its close), but he also relies for his opening and closing scenes, and for the most meaningful moments in between, on a wordless visual image brought to life through movement and dance. This is not a comfortable, sweetly nostalgic, or cathartic image, and it explains nothing away; rather it is a startling and visceral picture filled with energy and frustration – even rage. And it may be infectious, for of course it is not true that nobody is there to see it: effectively performed, the play's final image will haunt the imaginations of audiences for whom it might serve as a reminder of a still vibrant, angry, and powerful spirit realm. Audiences, indeed, might leave the theatre newly charged.

Works Cited

Taylor, Drew Hayden. *Girl Who Loved Her Horses. Staging Coyote's Dream: An Anthology of First Nations Drama in English*. Ed. Monique Mojica and Ric Knowles. Toronto: Playwrights Canada, 2003. 321-59.

———. "Introduction." *The Boy in the Treehouse* and *Girl Who Loved Her Horses*. Vancouver: Talonbooks, 1995. 5-6.

Interview with Drew Hayden Taylor

BIRGIT DÄWES AND ROBERT NUNN

The following consists of excerpts from two interviews with Drew Hayden Taylor. The first was conducted by Birgit Däwes on May 12, 2002 at the Ratskeller in Würzburg, Germany. The full text was published in *Contemporary Literature* (2003). The other was conducted by Robert Nunn on Dec. 21, 2004 at the Pauper's Pub in Toronto.

Däwes: Why do you think Native theatre is so much more successful in Canada than in the United States?

Taylor: I think this has a couple of reasons. It has to do with the representation. I think the Native voice is much more prevalent in Canadian society: we have very strong political representation, and we have very strong cultural and artistic representation in the larger Canadian mosaic. And I think Native people are the constant and predominant non-white presence available in Canada, whereas in the States it's the complete opposite. There are Native people there, but they are very fragmented; they don't have any unified voice, and there are other cultures that are more represented in the media than Native people. Take the example of African Americans and Native people and their representation in the dominant media in Canada and in the States. If you look at Canada, there have been – to the best of my knowledge – no television series that deal specifically with the black population, but there have been at least three dealing with the Native situation, as well as a very popular CBC radio show called "Dead Dog Café" [created by Thomas King, Floyd Favel Starr and Edna Rain] and the aboriginal voice in the past fifteen years has been amazingly strong and vital in the theatrical community.

Däwes: But why theatre – isn't that an unusual medium to have such an enormous success in our times?

Taylor: I have a theory of why Native theatre is so popular in general, and why it's popular in Canada: in the mid-1980s, it occurred to people that theatre is the next logical progression in traditional storytelling: the ability to take the audience on a journey using your voice, your body and the spoken word. Also the fact that unlike other media you don't need secondary knowledge.

Däwes: The annual festival of Native Earth Performing Arts Theatre Group . . .

Taylor: . . . Weesageechak Begins to Dance . . .

Däwes: ... was first organized in the late 1980s and seems to be have been highly influential in the rise and success of Native theatre in Canada. What is your own experience with that festival, and how do you evaluate its position in the theatre scene today?

Taylor: Well, I was only part of the first or the second festival, then missed a few. It used to be the only venue for the development of Native theatre in Canada during the late 1980s and early 1990s, but as I've often said, Native theatre has become so popular and caught on so much in Canada that almost every Native theatre company within every two to three years produces an existing Native play or develops one. You can get a Native play produced and workshopped almost everywhere in Canada today. So *Weesageechak* used to be the only game in town, now it's one of a lot of different games. It used to be Mount Everest, or even the only mountain, now it's one of several.

Däwes: Considering your own theatrical work, are there any playwrights, directors or theatre icons who have influenced you?

Taylor: Well, yes. More obviously, my mentor Larry Lewis, who used to be the Artistic Director of De-Ba-Jeh-Mu-Jig Theatre Group on Manitoulin Island, Ontario. He has degrees in literature and theatre and is very classically trained.

Although he is non-Native, he was, in my opinion, largely responsible for igniting the fire that became contemporary Native theatre. He dramaturged and directed all of Tomson Highway's work, as well as my first six plays. During my tenure, or what I refer to as my "mentorship" with De-Ba-Jeh-Mu-Jig from 1989 to 1991, I lived on Manitoulin Island in Wikwemikong with him, writing six plays for him in two years, and all were produced. I would not be who I am or where I am or what I am without Larry breathing down my neck those two years. And, to a certain extent, Tomson Highway. But our styles are so different, and while he's obviously the "grand fromage," the big guy, and he was instrumental in me getting my career and my job; I can't really say he influenced my writing, because we have two different styles. And in looking at non-Native writers, I found I really liked Eugene O'Neill, and to a certain extent, George Bernard Shaw.

Däwes: Since you mention O'Neill and Shaw – do your plays have a political agenda?

Taylor: I would say yes they do, because being born Native in Canada is a political statement in itself. So anything to do with an oppressed people and telling their story is bound to have some level of politics. I write different types of stories. In my comedies I make jokes about what happened at Oka and about race relations, cultural relations, political situations, drug and alcohol abuse, cultural loss, and a number of different things, and that is a political statement. So even though I often refer to my comedies as having no socially redeeming qualities whatsoever, that's an inaccurate assessment. And then I do what I call my "dramas," which are usually plays with a very strong social or political core to them, be it about Native adoption or cultural identity or something like *alterNatives,* which has a whole grab bag of issues involved in it. So I have to say the vast majority of my plays intentionally or non-intentionally have a strong political message somewhere within the text ...

Däwes: Those political questions seem to circle a lot around issues of authenticity and appropriation, and that is usually the case with literary discussions as well. There are voices in Native theatre (and literature in general) claiming that Native themes should only be put on stage by Natives. What is your position on that?

Taylor: That is a question that has been debated in the Native community for two decades now and my stance on that is: I have no problem with non-Native writers writing Native characters – I have too many unemployed Native actor friends who could use the work. And I have written white characters in my plays. The whole issue of appropriation is about where you draw the line: does that mean I can't write female characters, or Mohawk characters, etc.? What I may have a problem with is non-Native writers assuming a Native point of view for a story or writing a Native story. It's okay to have a Native character, have a Mexican character, have a German character, whatever you want, because in our everyday life we have these people coming into our lives and having a say in our lives and contributing to them, but at no point does that person start telling your story.

Däwes: Yes, the question of voice and the claim to "speak for" someone seem to play a crucial role for that decision. In "Reasons Why You Should be Nice to Native People" [*Further Adventures* 59-60] you take up these issues and mock non-Native tendencies to "try to 'out-Indian' Native people," or to "chase Native people around because they think there's a spiritual connection there somewhere." Are these examples exaggerated or is that something you actually encounter? And has anything changed about that since you wrote the article?

Taylor: The interesting thing is this modern recognition it receives in the Native communities. When *The Baby Blues* was produced in Tulsa, Oklahoma [by the Tulsa Indian Actors Theatre, with its premiere on May 25, 2000], the director [Merlaine Angwall] was white, from Wisconsin, and she really liked the Summer character. [Summer is a character in *The Baby Blues,* a naive non-Native woman who comes to a reserve in order to find spiritual guidance and to celebrate her own, peculiar notions of Native culture]. So Merlaine Angwall said "you know it's a really fun character to play, it's just a pity that it's a little over the top and not realistic." And then all the Native actors in Tulsa told her "oh no, it's not over the top, it's very very real." I also invited the cast of the premiere production in Toronto up to my pow wow, which was happening at the end of September, so the woman who was going to play Summer, a white actress, came up to the pow wow with us and there was this tall, blonde woman with blue eyes wearing a buckskin skirt and moccasins, dancing every intertribal and pow wow dance, you could just see her glowing with aboriginal pride. So, it's still existent there. I just reached a point in my life where I decided to look at it with more humor than annoyance.

Däwes: What's your experience in Germany concerning this issue?

Taylor: Not as much. I haven't really found the "new-ager, Summer influence" here, though people tell me that you guys have clubs and pow wows and festivals and stuff like that that deal with it, but I haven't seen it myself yet, so I can't really comment. But I have met so many people here who have a genuine interest in Native culture, which I'm more than happy to discuss.

Däwes: On the other hand, there is indeed a lot of stereotyping here in Germany, too. Most Germans grow up with the Winnetou myth from Karl May's novels and with the whole nineteenth-century stereotype of the "noble savage." These notions have a high market value, and there is a cult-like affinity between Germans and what they conceive of as "Indians." The German critic Hartmut Lutz has written extensively about this, and he coined the term "Indianthusiasm" to describe the phenomenon. Of course, on the academic level, there is also a more differentiated approach, and Native literature, for instance, is very popular among Germans. Have you had any personal experience with this German fascination with Native people?

Taylor: Obviously – I've been to three countries in Europe, I've been to Italy three times, to Belgium, and it's my fifth trip to Germany. Yet in all those countries – even when I go to the States – I never get asked to go on a lecture tour. But whenever I'm in Germany for a conference, I have to do a tour [of lectures and readings] afterwards. I find it very flattering, very intriguing, very unusual. Why there is this fascination, I don't know – it's probably a combination of everything from Karl May to the fact that Germans used to be very tribal themselves, the famous Roman legions battling the Germanic tribes of the Rhine and all that. I just think it's nice to see the genuine interest, and as I said, it's so different from any of the other European countries that I've been to, where they have a momentary interest in Native theatre; whereas here, I could probably tour [giving lectures and readings] for another week or two weeks easily.

Däwes: As with other stereotypes, you have frequently made fun of the image of the trickster as a stereotype. On the other hand, some of your characters do have trickster-like character traits. What is your position on trickster imagery in Native theatre?

Taylor: Daniel David Moses has a great quote about how academics seem to believe that nothing can be Native unless it has trickster imagery in it. And so, he has coined this term: the "spot-the-trickster syndrome." I tend to find it annoying, because when I used to run *Native Earth [Performing Arts]* I had to read all these scripts, and I would story-edit movies, and it got to the point where Native people started to believe that any story they wanted to write couldn't be told without some form of trickster imagery in it, and it just got ridiculous after a while, so – other than a movie script I wrote which I'm hoping to turn into a book called "Motorcycles and Sweetgrass" – I've tried to avoid trickster imagery completely, just because again, I think it's another overused cliché.

Däwes: In your preface to *Boy in the Treehouse,* you wrote that *Girl Who Loved Her Horses* is your favorite of all the plays you have written. Is that still the case?

Taylor: Oh yeah. But that's a tough question, because it's like saying "who's your favorite child?" if you have eight or nine children. You really can't say because each one is something special to you. *Toronto at Dreamer's Rock* was my first play, and my most successful, *alterNatives* I think is my most complicated play, so I'm proud of that, *Only Drunks and Children Tell the Truth* strikes on a really unique emotional level and has also been one of my most successful plays, but when I sit down and read them, *Girl Who Loved Her Horses* is the only play that makes me sit there and think "Wow! I wrote that!" It strikes me on a completely different level. Because it's the only play I've written that makes me feel like an artist.

Däwes: Please tell me something about how you write – about your creative process and how your ideas are turned into plays.

Taylor: The creative process varies from project to project. In a case like *Girl Who Loved Her Horses,* the idea came from a story one of my best friends told me, a non-Native woman named Danielle, who was raised in an urban, white environment. Her mother would invite kids over to draw on her wall. And Danielle told me of this little girl who would show up, a white shy little girl who would draw a horse week after week until one day she just stopped coming. And she said they always wondered about that, and the image stuck in my head. And then my creative process was like the way language functions in Ojibway, where you have the root word, and you add bits to it, and it gets bigger and bigger until I actually had a story.

With my comedies, it's easier when I start with a humorous situation. So when I was doing *The Bootlegger Blues,* I remembered a story that happened on my reserve and I ended up pumping it up and then I had a play. And then with *The Baby Blues,* I first developed a character and then created the worst possible type of environment I could for that character. *Someday* came from interesting origins when I noticed that I knew or I made friends with and met a lot of Native adoptees. And then I found out about the scoop-up, when Native kids were taken away for adoption by their [Canadian] federal government and I was absolutely amazed by the fact that nobody knew about it. And I thought, well this might make an interesting story. So my work in process is either taking a visual image or a specific idea and then just adding on to it, developing it, giving it a beginning, a middle, and an end.

Däwes: And do you work at several projects at the same time?

Taylor: Kind of. I may have two or three projects juggling, but when I sit down to write, I will write a draft all the way through, because I'm what's called a "momentum writer." I have to pick up speed as I'm writing, or I'll lose the thread of what I'm trying to say. But once I get it down, I can always come back to it later, so when I have one project in front of me I tend to focus my entire attention on it.

Däwes: In another conversation, you have talked about the "ingredients" of the creative process and how they sometimes turn out differently in the reading or staging. How does this apply to your work?

Taylor: I've come to the conclusion over the years that in terms of what people read into a play, text and subtext, a third is intentional, a third is unconscious – which means that I know I have to get this idea, this image or this feeling across, but I'm not sure exactly why or how. And then a third of it is just completely accidental, a complete fluke. I'm always puzzled and amused by English teachers and professors and students who read and analyze my works and works of other writers and get all the sort of subtextual stuff in there that may or may not be there and that always amuses me. I remember bumping into a woman who was doing a research paper on *Only Drunks and Children Tell the Truth,* and she was complimenting me on the use of the name Janice for the adoptee character. She said, "Well, I just think it's a great metaphor, using Janice in terms of the Roman two-faced God Janus." This is a great idea and I would love to take credit for that but I can't. That was just a complete fluke.

Däwes: You once said that when you write your plays, your characters actually do the work for you. How exactly does that work?

Taylor: As a writer I've worked on plays when neither the story nor the characters have been developed. And over the years I find that the more finely tuned your characters are, the more three-dimensional they are, the easier it is to write a play, because if they are as real as the world around you, they will help you with your writing and even write a large percentage of your play for you. There have been many situations when I've been backed into a corner, trying to figure out where I'm going to go with a scene, and I don't know what to do. Then I just sit down and think about the character as a real person, with certain preferences and skills, and I try to imagine what he or she would do. And when I sit there, they come up with an idea and I'll be saved. It always works, and it's so fulfilling when you know that your characters are on your side, that you don't have to push your characters but sometimes they push you.

Däwes: That sounds like a moment of satisfaction, you know, a moment when, more than at any other time, we know exactly why we do what we do. Do you remember any other such moment during a production or during the process of writing, when being a writer just felt particularly good?

Taylor: Well, it could be when I got the cheque for $10,000! [The Chalmers Canadian Play Award in 1992]. *[Laughter.]* But yes, every once in a while something really unusual throws me out of my normal complacency loop and shows me what can be done. After *Bootlegger [Blues]*, when *Someday* was staged, I saw people crying in the audience and realized that in addition to humour and making people laugh, I had the ability to make people cry. I felt a weird type of pride, knowing that this manipulation of emotion is possible.

Däwes: And how about in a negative sense – have you ever had a reaction from an audience that made you angry or that you didn't understand at all?

Taylor: I didn't understand the bomb threat I got for *alterNatives* in Vancouver. [The production of *alterNatives* in Vancouver received a bomb threat in 1999 for its alleged "racism against white people"]. That was such a negative response and I don't understand that. Also, a Native woman came up to me and said, "Is this what you really think of Native people?" and so I get responses like that, but everybody is entitled to an opinion, and you just have to accept that and move on ...

Däwes: This is going to be a difficult question, but as a playwright, where would you see your position within the larger scene of Native arts, or your contribution to it?

Taylor: As a Native playwright, I just want to tell some interesting stories with interesting characters that take the audience on a journey. As for my own contribution, I hope that I have provided a window of understanding between

Native and non-Native cultures by demystifying Native life. For Native people, I have provided an opportunity to see themselves on stage. I ask a few questions, hopefully provide a few answers, and we have some fun along the way.

Däwes: If you were an art sponsor and had enormous financial possibilities, what would you do for Native theatre?

Taylor: In a perfect world, I would love to start my own theatre company and do three shows a season. I'd like to do one new, brand new Native play that we develop, I would like to do a remount of some existing Native play, and I would like to do an aboriginal interpretation of an existing non-Native play. For instance, my Brecht/Weill play [an "Indianization" of Brecht's *The Rise and Fall of the City of Mahagonny* entitled "Sucker Falls: A Musical About the Demons of the Forest and the Soul" planned for 2003]. Or, Tomson Highway has always wanted to direct *A Streetcar Named Desire,* Elizabeth Theobald [Cherokee; the Director of Public Programs at the Mashantucket Pequot Museum and Research Center in Rhode Island and the director of several productions of Drew Taylor's plays] has always wanted to do a Native and French Canadian version of *Henry V* based on what happened at

Oka, a company in Terrace, BC wants to do *Romeo and Juliet* from a white and Native perspective, and there are so many other wonderful plays out there. I'd love to do Native adaptations of existing plays . . .

*

Nunn: I'm going to start with a few quotes from your video about Native humour, *Redskins, Tricksters and Puppy Stew*. I'd like to ask you to treat them as a jazz musician might treat them, and riff on them. I'll start with Tom King:

> I'm dealing with cultural humour. And occasionally I'm going to hold that mirror up to white Canada, and say, "See, this is what it feels like." You can get in the front door with humour. You can get into the kitchen with humour. If you're pounding on the front door they won't let you in. They may gather the kids around to watch you on the front stoop making a fool of yourself sometimes. Which doesn't mean I don't believe in that sort of confrontational activism, but it's just not me. It's not what I'm good at. Humour is . . . I'm better at humour.

Taylor: I find that you can often achieve both objectives with humour. Humour can be very biting, humour can pound on the door, humour is very confrontational. The thing about humour too is, ninety percent of all humour is at somebody's expense. But the great thing about humour is it sugar-coats it. It sugar-coats issues, criticisms, it makes uncomfortable topics comfortable. What you can say in anger that would be objectionable you might be able to say in a humourous manner that would not be as objectionable. And also humour works from the bottom up. I'm talking about the social status, and ladders. That is to say, it is not possible, or I'm told it's not possible, for white people to make fun of people further on down the social ladder. It only works crossways and up; so as a Native person I can make fun of white people, black people can make fun of white people, Asians can make fun of white people, but white people in today's politically correct times cannot make fun of Native people, black people, or people of any other marginalized culture. So what he talks about here – "I'm going to hold that mirror up to white culture, and say, see, this is what it feels like" – that's often the focus of humour, it turns the tables around and puts the person in the other set of shoes.

Nunn: Have you got feedback from white spectators that yeah, I see things differently after I saw your play?

Taylor: Not really. I have had feedback from white people. And ninety-nine times out of a hundred it's all been positive. I sometimes worry when I'm writing stuff that maybe I'm being too Native. In many of my plays I think there's a good percentage of Indian jokes that only Indians will get. However, having been artistic director of Native Earth, I was faced with the reality that there's approximately three million people in the Toronto area; of that, seventy thousand may be Native. Of that seventy thousand maybe one to two hundred will go and see a play. So I do a three-week run of a play here in Toronto and let's face it, that one to two hundred people will not pay the bills. So the plays that we write have to be cross-cultural, and have to be able to be appreciated by a non-Native audience. So when I'm doing a comedy I don't sit down and try to make my stories cross-cultural or make the humour appreciable by non-Native people, because the same things that make us laugh make you laugh. I go home, I watch *The Simpsons,* I watch *Friends,* I love them, I laugh. Humour is universal, just like drama is universal, that's why they're still doing Shakespeare today four hundred years afterwards, that's why in some places they're still doing the Greek comedies. The best metaphor I ever came up with was, let's say humour is like chicken: there are a thousand different ways to cook chicken, adding different spices, different herbs, but it's still chicken. Same with humour. Native humour, Jewish humour, black humour: I know sitting in front of the television watching black comedians I get the humour, I get the humour on the level of being part of a marginalized culture, I get the humour being North American, sometimes they use that kind of broad spectrum humour; so I'm a firm believer that humour is cross-cultural and that regardless of what I write, in terms of writing jokes and humour, there's no particularly Native way to boil an egg.

Nunn: Tom King again.

> ...those things that hurt in life, those things that continue to hurt about being Native in North America. I can handle those things through humour. I can't handle those through anger because, I get angry about something and it just gets away from me. It just consumes me. And so I've gotta keep coming back to humour as my sort of my safe position. And I think I make more of an impact...

Taylor: Anger is good, it's made a lot of change in the world, but I agree with Tom here, that sometimes anger may not be the best way to deal with something.

Nunn: What makes you really angry, that you would rather not say outright but would get at through humour?

Taylor: What makes me really angry? The normal stuff that makes all of us really angry, social injustice, poverty, all that sort of stuff. But I'm not an angry person. I never have been. I've seen anger do more damage in my life than it's done good for people, I've seen fights, I've seen women and children hiding from drunk fathers, I've seen fights start for the stupidest reason, and I've just never really understood it, so I purposely never really developed a sense of anger. Which has often been problematic with many of the partners I've had in my life because they often expressed themselves through anger, and I wouldn't, and that would infuriate them: the fact that I would prefer to deal with issues through humour rather than anger. I would make a joke to try and defuse the situation.

Nunn: Next: Herbie Barnes:

> I find a lot of the Native humour is an exploration of the dark side. Like *[deep voice]* "Come over to the dark side, Luke." A lot of our humour stems around our tragedies that happen. We joke about that, and it's partly our survival technique. So I think that that's a big part of what it is. We look at ... we don't only laugh at the guy who slips on the banana peel, but it's a lot funnier if he breaks his leg, I think, for us.

Taylor: Well, Native humour, much like Jewish humour, is survival humour. It comes from survival stories. If you look at the early years of the contemporary Native literary renaissance, most of the stories written by and about Native people were dark, angry, depressing, bleak, because, using Tomson Highway's famous saying, "Before the healing can take place, the poison must be exposed." And I think when an oppressed people get their voice back, they will write about being oppressed. So the first generation of writers: they were talking about that oppression, they were writing about the pain, the anger, the travesties, and the things that we were overcoming, this is what has happened to us in the last five hundred years, this is what we're dealing with. And when I was in India, just right now there is a growing birth of *dalit* literature, *dalit* being the untouchables, formerly called the untouchables, who are now writing their stories, and I met a few of them down there, and these stories, much like the earlier Native stories, are dark and angry, talking about being at the bottom of the caste system. So there's not a lot of humour there. And I think it's a progressional thing. Most black literature started off being dark, angry, depressing, accusatory, stuff like that, because, as Tomson says, the poison has to be exposed before the healing can take place. And I think every literature, every people reaches a point of ... it's like stars, right, you have all this gas coming in and it gets bigger and bigger and it reaches a point where there is a spark that brings the sun to life, based on the amount of gravity, the amount of mass and all that that starts it going. And I think it's the same here, that we've gone through enough . . . any people who go through enough of a cathartic process, in talking about these depressing stories, the healing will take place. A Blood Elder from the Blood Reserve in Alberta said "Humour is the WD-40 of healing." And I believe that. So in terms of what Herbie's saying about the dark side, yes, a lot of our humour comes from a way of dealing with the tragedies of the past five hundred years of colonization. I remember hearing this funny story: somewhere up in the North, an Inuit man was watching his house burn down, and he was laughing, and the white guy came over and said, "Your house is burning down, why are you laughing?" And he said, "Because if I become angry or cry, it will embarrass my neighbours as to my situation. So if I laugh, they will feel better." Hmm. Almost makes sense.

Nunn: Yeah. Almost. It's very difficult to jump into that way of thinking, but it's more important to be part of the community than to stand there and cry over your . . .

Taylor: Right. Exactly. It's the same thing with Native theatre and a lot of the way Tomson Highway writes: the fact that the community is more important than the individual. Tomson had great difficulties getting his first two plays produced by mainstream theatre companies, because there's no central character. Looking at most plays like *The Iceman Cometh,* or any of Shakespeare, there's a central character or two central characters that everything revolves around. You know, the famous protagonist-antagonist type of concept. Whereas Tomson wrote ensemble pieces, and many Native writers write ensemble pieces because community's more important than the individual. There is no star in a community.

Nunn: I think that applies to your stuff too.

Taylor: To a certain extent. In *The Baby Blues,* Noble is a central character, and everything revolves around Noble. But you've got *Someday,* you've got *Only Drunks and Children Tell the Truth,* you've got *Buz'Gem Blues, alterNatives,* yeah, it is ensemble in nature.

Nunn: Don Burnstick:

> . . . it wasn't a very long time ago that our people were in a lot of despair, eh? just in my own life, and now to come to this place of this laughing, and that spirit, and being so strong . . . you know the humour started coming back so strong with our people, it's just a great feeling to be a part of that, you know? to be a tool you know. It's just awesome you know and I'm grateful for that, for being a tool that's gonna facilitate this process eh, because we went through our whole, like let's have empowerment, let's heal, let's sober up, let's do this, and now we're at this place where we're really laughing . . . celebrating . . .

Taylor: About two months ago I was invited to participate in a night of Native humour, Native comedy, at the Kennedy Center in Washington D.C. I was asked to introduce and open for Don Burnstick and Charlie Hill, two leading Native comedians in North America, and we did two shows, and it was a room *full* of love, both shows. And this was my first experiment with standup, and I only had to do five-ten minutes, they did about half an hour each, and it went very very well; and just looking at that room, thinking, here we are at the Kennedy Center, we are launching this new museum [the National Museum of the American Indian, Washington, D.C., which opened on September 21, 2004], and it was sort of like, wow, everything was so positive there that it left you with a really good feeling.

Nunn: Anything more you want to riff on that?

Taylor: Well, Don Burnstick's own personal story: he was a drug addict, an alcoholic who cleaned himself up, went out and made a negative into a positive. He used the pain to be a place of strength for his humour. The two pictures of the two masks of Greek theatre, comedy and tragedy, they're just flip sides of each other. It's like the opposite of love is not hate, it's indifference. Love and hate are actually quite closely entwined. You know, you see a couple that really hate each other, chances are they really loved each other. So it's the same with the humour coming from tragedy. I've been to funerals where we had really good laughs, nothing disrespectful to the family or the person who died, but it's just our way; we find humour in everything, we celebrate life through humour. When I die I want a good Irish wake.

Nunn: A student in Herbie Barnes' improv class says:

> Humour is transforming. It can take you to another place . . . good, bad, ugly . . . things you want to hide or things you want to celebrate, because I come from a tradition where even in ceremony, where that is the most crucial, most serious part of our lives, there's joke telling, there's people playing the trickster, showing their comic wit, and I think that is distinctly Native, because I would not find that in a Catholic church or a Protestant church or a . . . they weren't doing that when I visited the Vatican . . . they weren't cracking jokes or having a good time.

Taylor: You realize in the Bible nowhere does it say Jesus ever smiled or laughed. It says he cried, he wept, never laughed. What little I know of the various denominations of the Christian belief, they're not really geared towards having a good time or laughing. Having been to a hundred and twenty Native communities, having been in all sorts of ceremonies and places like that, the humour is very very persuasive. There's nothing like sitting around and just telling funny story after funny story after funny story wherever you are. The funny thing is, if you get two groups — a group of non-Native people and a group of Native people — chances are the Native people will start laughing almost immediately and more frequently and louder than any other group of people, I think, in my opinion, but then I'm slightly biassed.

Nunn: But that thing about humour being part of spiritual life . . .

Taylor: The clowns of the . . . is it the Hopi or the Pueblo? When they have a ceremony somebody's delegated to be the clown, and he comes out and he's all painted up, in clothes that are horizontally striped. And their function in these ceremonies is to come out, and the kids and the adults laugh at him, and he's supposed to be very funny but his purpose also is to point out people and issues that are in danger of bringing disharmony to the community. If they think somebody's getting too high and mighty, too greedy, or doing something that's interfering with the harmony of the community they will take that person and make fun of them in front of everybody else, and it's a great social adjusting metaphor. Their function is to maintain the harmony of the community by humbling those that need to be humbled.

Nunn: Maybe asking you about Native humour has a whiff of pan-Indianism. As if humour was the same across the spectrum of all the First Nations. Is there something that's specifically Ojibway about Ojibway humour?

Taylor: Whenever I talk about Native humour I often acknowledge the fact that that's a very pan-Indianistic term. At time of contact I think there were over fifty separate languages and dialects spoken in Canada, and oftentimes each dialect, each language, denotes a certain type of humour. And often it's been my experience that humour can change from community to community, let alone from nation to nation. But there are certain universal factors I find in the world of Native humour. First of all there are two dominant characteristics of Native humour regardless of the pan-Indian aspect: one is that the humour is self-deprecatory. We tend to make fun of ourselves as individuals, as a nation or as all nations. Don Burnstick's humour is all self-deprecatory. He makes fun of himself, about Crees, about anything, constantly. And again I think that's a great levelling thing about keeping the social structure in place. The other dominant characteristic of Native humour is teasing. Native people love to tease, and oftentimes it shows that when you're being teased by a community, you have been accepted into that community, because it is impolite to tease a stranger, at least to his face. There's even an anthropological term for that type of teasing; it's called "permitted disrespect." Now that being said, the humour does vary from nation to nation. I find that some cultures have a very aggressive, very in-your-face sense of humour such that oftentimes you don't know, when somebody has told you a joke, or teased you, whether to laugh or punch them out. Now with other cultures like the Ojibway and the Cree I find the humour is often so subtle, it's so what I like to call around-the-corner humour, that you don't know somebody's made a joke until they themselves start laughing. It can be very deadpan.

Nunn: Which brings me to the next question. In an interview you once said, "I think the way I write is a result of my upbringing. Growing up on the reserve, I was surrounded by this marvellous sense of humour. I have a reputation as a humourist, but I'm no match for some of my uncles and aunts." Can you elaborate on that?

Taylor: I think everybody in my community is actually quite funny. But the interesting thing is, oftentimes I don't recognize it. Whenever I used to bring any of my girlfriends or friends home they'd say my mother is very funny, but I don't find my mother to be particularly funny. Yet people say she is. And when I told her I was going to do this night of Native comedy at the Kennedy Center in Washington she looked at me really surprised and said, "Well, you'd better learn to be funny then."

Nunn: Sounds like round-the-corner humour.

Taylor: No, she was deadly serious She was deadly serious. So oftentimes I guess it just shows we don't see what's in our own backyard. I find most of my aunts and uncles hilariously funny, that kind of wonderful broad rez humour that can be dirty, that can be sexy, that can be very very taunting. I find it very very refreshing, and oftentimes I go home just to recharge my humour batteries.

Nunn: Larry Lewis challenged you, didn't he, to write *The Bootlegger Blues*. "Write me a comedy." Why did he pick you?

Taylor: Well, at that time there were only three working Native playwrights in Ontario. There were Tomson Highway, Daniel David Moses and me. And Dan Moses, as much as I admire him, is not really known for his comedy. Tomson can be deadly funny, but Tomson is a slow writer, and he does his own schtick so to speak. I just did my very first play, called *Toronto at Dreamer's Rock:* I knew nothing of theatre, I sat down, I wrote it, with Larry hovering over me, and I thought it was a complete failure because

I didn't know theatre, I didn't like theatre, and I thought the play was crap, I thought it was overly issue-oriented, it was very straight, wasn't funny. And when I would go see it performed, people were laughing, and I couldn't figure out why, I said it's not that funny. And then Larry had just done a remount of *Dry Lips Oughta Move to Kapuskasing,* and he came back and said, "Drew, I think Native theatre has got too serious. We need to do something about this, so I want you to go and write me something that doesn't have people drying their eyes from crying too much, or scratching their head from thinking too much, I want them to be holding their stomachs from having laughed too much. I want you to write something that celebrates the Native sense of humour." So I went out and I wrote *The Bootlegger Blues,* and I often say it's a comedy with absolutely no socially redeeming qualities whatsoever. And we didn't know if it would be successful or not, because nobody had ever seen a Native comedy before, let alone one about bootlegging. I guess Larry saw my humour because I'd done one other play with him before then, a play that was never produced, called "Up the Road," where after the workshop in Toronto I took it into the backyard, put a bullet through the title page and buried it. But I guess he saw that I loved to play with words and play with concepts, and he just said, "Let's go, let's go have some fun and do a comedy." And it's been pretty good so far.

Nunn: A lot of your humour is pointed, and it can overturn stereotypes, but it's never cruel. When you're making fun of somebody it's never the whole story. I felt that was the case with Summer. She's wonderful, and very ridiculous, but she's also got feelings that all this ridiculous behaviour comes from, and you respect those feelings. And the audience gets to see them, so that they have a kind of stereoscopic view of the character; they're laughing at them but they have a sense of where they're coming from.

Taylor: Yes, I was always taught humour should amuse, not abuse. What you're saying is essentially correct. It almost got to the point where somebody commented that all the characters I've ever written were very sympathetic, that I'd never written a bad and evil or an unsympathetic character. So I sat down and I wrote *alterNatives,* in which I thought all the characters were deeply flawed, and while at the end two characters manage to slightly redeem themselves, you know that they're still very flawed and you don't know where this is going to go or what's going to happen. The interesting thing about Summer is she's often perceived as being silly or stupid or the ultimate wannabe, but the thing people forget is, she's also very intelligent. I mean she's going through university, she speaks better English than most of us do, and she's very bright. The only flaw I find in her is her enthusiasm. She's way too enthusiastic, and you know it'd drive you up the wall. But I try and love all my characters and give them that double-edged sword of being silly but tinging it with a bit of, if not melancholy, a bit of darkness that gives them a reason: because we're never born the way we are, we're made the way we are, and it's always nice to find out what makes our characters the way they are.

Nunn: It would have been very easy to just make fun of the wannabe, and nail her to the wall, but you know, she's a wannabe for a reason, she's trying to find out who she is.

Taylor: Yeah, victims aren't funny.

Nunn: That's right, the more you nail them to the wall, the less funny they are, even though you accomplished the purpose. There's more to it than that.

Taylor: As long as they fight back, and defend themselves, they're fine.

Nunn: And she's capable of defending herself.

Taylor: Oh yeah, she's way smarter than Noble, way smarter than Skunk, she's better off than most of them. In *The Baby Blues,* she's being chased by all the guys, and she finally ends up with the smart one, the Elder. So she's no dummy. And she's also one of my favourite characters. As I say, when I was writing *The Bootlegger Blues,* I fell in love with Noble. 'Cause he was a minor character, but everything he said and every place he was and all that was very very funny; he had such a dry pithy way of surreally looking at the world around him, and I just fell in love with him; I thought I want to do a play around him, so I ended up doing *The Baby Blues* and putting him in the worst possible position I could. And then there I created Summer, and Summer was just so fabulous that I wanted to see what I could do with her next. And I couldn't bring Summer back without bringing Amos back. So Summer is very close to my heart. She's a sweetie.

Nunn: You've been called the Neil Simon of Native playwrights. How do you respond to that? Is there somebody else you'd rather be called?

Taylor: Oh God yes, I've been called the Neil Simon of Native plays for the last ten years. Ever since *The Bootlegger Blues* came out. It's not an insult. A lot of people think it's an insult, but I like his early stuff, *Barefoot in the Park, The Odd Couple,* they're brilliantly structured, he's very wealthy, and . . . I'm just curious why there's the need to categorize me as . . . categorize me period, let alone as Neil Simon. I mean there are other people out there who write comedies, not just me.

Nunn: Certain of your plays seem to be able to turn on a dime from laughter to tears. How close together are those emotions to you? How important is it to you to bring those emotions together?

Taylor: Well, as I said earlier about the twin masks of Greek theatre, comedy and tragedy: I think they are perfectly entwined, and the ability to use them that way is I think a very important trait. I love doing dramas and I love doing comedies. Doing comedies is like a big bowl of popcorn, it's just so much fun to do and I couldn't imagine not wanting to do comedies, but comedies get very little respect for some reason. I enjoy doing that, but I agree with your comment about the ability to turn on a dime: there's been a couple of instances where it happens in my plays. I'll give you an example. The end of Act One in *Someday* when Janice is driving up in the car, and they [Rodney, Barb and Anne] are looking out through the window, following her coming up – and this is the long lost daughter who was scooped up, returning home after thirty-five years – and

Rodney's describing her coming up the driveway and going into the ditch, and she gets out and starts walking, and the mother can't look and then finally she says she has to see, and she gets up and walks over and says "I don't see her, where is she?" And Rodney says, "She's disappeared." And the mother goes, "Not again." And you can just hear the hearts in the audience, both laugh and squeezed like that.

Nunn: About popular culture: the gag about the professor and Marianne [as in *Gilligan's Island*] is so nicely set up in *The Buz'Gem Blues*, it takes a moment to realize what you're actually witnessing; and there are the *Star Trek* references in the same play; and there is the Amelia Earhart thing which I thought was fabulous [in *Only Drunks and Children Tell the Truth* we are told that the famous American aviatrix didn't die in the plane wreck but found her way to the Otter Lake reserve where she has been living incognito ever since]. Where does that come from, this kind of fun with popular culture?

Taylor: Well, we're all products of popular culture. Forty years ago almost all the references you'd find in literature, radio and television were either from the Bible or Shakespeare. Today it's a completely different world, and it's become very incestuous, references feed on themselves, over and over, mutate, come out with new, with completely different references. Nowadays people quote *Star Trek* and *The Simpsons* and other things like that, so even though I didn't really see television until I was seven, we're products of this pop culture and it permeates everyday life. So you can't ignore the pop cultural world out there. Now the thing with Amelia Earhart: that just came because I wanted to add a bit of surrealism to *Only Drunks and Children Tell the Truth*. And it's also a reference to many Native communities: there are always one or two white people somewhere on the reserve, usually by themselves, and you have no idea how they got there, but they just happen to be there. So I wanted to use that as a reference. And as to *Star Trek:* I used to be a Trekkie, and it's just fun. I like combining the two cultures, stuff in the Native community, stuff in the dominant community, bringing them together and seeing what happens. One of my favourite jokes is in *alterNatives* when Dale asks Angel if he was a Trekkie, and he says, "Only half, on my mother's side."

Nunn: About audience response: when I saw *The Baby Blues* at Theatre Passe Muraille, there was quite a mixed audience of Native and non-Native. Everybody was just roaring with laughter, but I'm sure there were bits where Native people were laughing more than non-Natives, and I could feel that. It's an interesting experience for a non-Native person to say, "Hey, there's something here that I'm not quite getting."

Taylor: You've heard me say that a play must be accessible to all people. For me to write a play specifically for a Native audience would be very self-defeating and in the end very expensive. But there's certainly a universality in story-telling. *Someday* is about a woman who lost her child to the Children's Aid Society thirty-five years ago and is waiting for her to come back. The characters are Native, the story is Native, the issue's Native, and the community's Native, but there's no particularly Native way for a mother to love her child. It's the same with humour. Some of the jokes in *The Baby Blues:* about growing old, everybody can relate to that; trying to pick up a hot chick, everybody can relate to that; everybody knows somebody like Noble, who refuses to grow up, regardless of the culture; so there is that universality involved. However, as you heard me say earlier, there are certain jokes that Native people either appreciate more or understand more than a non-Native person would. One of the best examples was when they did *The Buz'Gem Blues* in Port Dover: the Woodland

Cultural Centre [on the Six Nations Reserve] had a fund-raising evening, where they bought out the house for ten dollars a ticket and then they sold the ticket for twenty. So in that house, which seats three hundred people, I think they managed to sell two hundred tickets. There were two hundred Native people in there. The play ran normally about an hour and forty-five minutes without the intermission. That night it ran eight minutes longer, just from laughter. Regular audiences laughed a lot, but the Native audience added an extra eight minutes to the run of that show.

In the premiere of *In a World Created by a Drunken God,* there was a handful of Native people in the audience, and they laughed at one joke that none of the audience really laughed at: one of the characters is packing up to move, and he's putting all his t-shirts in boxes and garbage bags, he's folding them quite neatly, and the other character's commenting on how many Native-themed t-shirts he has, and he says with a shrug, "I go to a lot of conferences." And the Native people all burst out laughing, 'cause that's what we do: we've gone from following the buffalo to following the conference trail. Maria Campbell was in the audience, and she was telling me afterwards she has a bottom drawer full of t-shirts from all the conferences she's been to. She never wears them, because she doesn't wear t-shirts. She doesn't want to give them away 'cause they're gifts, but she just has this huge pile of conference t-shirts that she doesn't know what to do with. So a dozen Indians in the audience laughed at that joke.

Nunn: Didn't you say once too that non-Native audiences at a comedy written about and by Native people have to be reassured that it's okay to laugh?

Taylor: Yeah, they're looking for permission to laugh. I don't know if it's so much so today, but at one point when we were doing *The Bootlegger Blues* in Port Dover in 1993, the audience was slow to laugh because they didn't think they should laugh at Native people. Political correctness told them that you're not to laugh at Native people doing a play about alcohol. So luckily Port Dover is right next to the Six Nations Reserve, and there were maybe about a dozen people from Six Nations in there, and they were howling. And about ten or fifteen minutes into the play, it took the audience about that long to sit up and say, oh, it's a comedy, we can laugh at this, we have permission to laugh at this. So they did. Now I think with the success of *Smoke Signals* and other plays and my work, and Tom King's humour, I think there's less of a reluctance to laugh, there's more of an acceptance.

Nunn: Could you talk about your creative process with specific regard to humour, what state of mind works best for you to get comic situations and dialogue flowing?

Taylor: It's always important to have your characters write their own funny lines. One of the things I learned in doing *The Bootlegger Blues* was that it wasn't enough to come up with six different characters, I had to come up with six different senses of humour. I had to figure out a way of giving each character a way to make the audience laugh. That was a great learning experience for me, that's continued on in my writing. So some of the characters are very deadpan, and they deliver their line without trying to be funny; and then you get the snarky, cocky characters that are purposely trying to be funny; and then you have other people that are somewhere in the middle: and so you have to find the shades of grey, to make your characters have a different sense of humour, so that you can look at a joke and figure out which of these characters would have said it. And sometimes the humour comes right off the bat. Usually there's a process when I'm writing a play, a three step process. The first draft is to tell the story, second draft is to develop the characters, and third draft is to make sure the story and the characters are working together. So oftentimes I'm sitting down and I'm writing something, and there'll be a certain amount of humour in it, but you add more humour with each draft because you're fine-tuning the characters, you're fine-tuning the characters' interpretation of that universe, and finding a way of building the humour towards the big payoff.

Now with the articles and essays, that's a different process. The best way to describe the humour in my articles and essays is to say that I just re-invent reality. I take a reality that I've seen out there that the Creator has done, and I look at its absurdities. I'm a firm believer that God, the Creator, whatever term you wish to use, has a great sense of humour, and it's just that most of us are not tempted to see it; and I've trained myself over the years to watch the world around me and pick up God's one-liners. And I manage to use them in my articles and essays. And let me tell you, God's a great co-writer.

Nunn: *Someday, Only Drunks and Children Tell the Truth,* and *400 Kilometres* deal with the heartbreaking subject of the scoop-up of Native children for adoption by non-Natives. And I am willing to bet that those plays, and the short story on the front page of the *Globe and Mail* that started it all [reprinted in *Fearless Warriors*], shocked a lot of white people into awareness of terrible harm done to Native communities by institutions they support with their taxes. Yet the plays are funny, and touching, and possibly even healing. Are there any aspects of the "five hundred years of oppression" that you feel you couldn't write a play like *Someday* about?

Taylor: I don't think the world is ready for a humourous residential school story, yet. It's kinda hard to make fun of children's sexual abuse. Not that anybody would want to. So I think there are still some areas that are taboo, that are still sensitive. Especially, the whole concept of political correctness: somebody who's never been to residential school finding the humour in such situations might not be correct. Tomson [Highway] could probably do it, he's been to residential school, and he often has a very dark sense of humour. Someday that will happen. I have an idea in my head for a residential school story. Provided I have the time and the interest, I am going to write it. Who knows, I might be able to find some nuggets of humour in there.

Nunn: Basil Johnston has written that if tribal languages die (e.g. if Anishinaubae is no longer a living language spoken by Ojibway people) Native people "lose not only the ability to express the simplest of daily sentiments and needs but they can no longer understand the ideas, concepts, insights, attitudes, rituals, ceremonies, institutions brought into being by their ancestors; and, having lost the power to understand, cannot sustain, enrich, or pass on their heritage. No longer will they think Indian or feel Indian... They will have lost their identity" (99-100). I felt that in your plays there is such a variety of speakers of Native languages: some like Martha [in *The Bootlegger Blues* and *The Buz'Gem Blues*] are birthright speakers of Ojibway, but there are others who have learned it for one reason or another like Janice [in *400 Kilometres*] or Summer [in *The Baby Blues* and *The Buz'Gem Blues*], and so it's a very complicated issue in your plays. I wonder if you wanted to comment on it.

Taylor: It is a complicated issue 'cause it's a complicated issue in my life. Using the quote by James Joyce, I'm forced to write in a conqueror's tongue. I explore this in an essay I wrote ["From the PEN International Conference on Indigenous Languages in Mexico City," *Funny # 4* 10-13] where I talked about what I referred to as the dog syndrome, where you tell a dog to roll over, the dog hears you, it understands, it rolls over. But it cannot respond to you in the same manner in which you originated the instruction. So my mother tells me to turn the kettle on. I hear her, I understand, and I turn the kettle on, but I cannot respond to my mother in the manner in which she commanded me. So it's an issue I go through in my own life. I understand more Ojibway than I speak, but when I put Ojibway in my plays, I have to go to either my aunt, Anita Nott, or somebody here in Toronto, Isidore Toulouse, to ask for translations to put in my plays. And I feel very self-conscious about doing that. I agree with Basil: there's an old saying, the voice of our land is in our language. And the way you express yourself, the words you choose, the grammar you choose, are often indicative of a thought process and a cultural process in which that language was created. So when that dies it becomes replaced by another foreign language. I do think a large chunk of that Native identity is gone. I don't know if I agree with Basil that everything is gone but I do think a good chunk of the identity has been replaced.

Nunn: That's the tough situation where you are. You understand Ojibway but you don't speak it fluently.

Taylor: Exactly.

Nunn: So you're there, you can hear that different cultural approach but you can't speak it.

Taylor: Right. So it's difficult. And it's very interesting: my mother told me that she learned English when she was eleven or twelve. About twelve years ago, when she was about sixty and

I was thirty, she said, "I've been speaking English for fifty years, and you've only been speaking it for less than thirty, how come you're so much better at it than I am? I don't understand it." And I said, "'Cause, mum, you think in Ojibway, Ojibway is your first language; when you speak English, you're unconsciously translating from Ojibway into English. So it's a major hiccup for you."

Nunn: Probably you could feel the influence of Ojibway syntax.

Taylor: Ojibway's a gender neutral language; there are no hims and hers, hes and shes. They only change in tense. Something is either active or inactive, something is either alive or not alive. So my mother to this day after speaking English for sixty years still gets hims and hers and hes and shes completely screwed up.

Nunn: In Maria Campbell's *Stories of the Road Allowance People* it's the same thing. You do a double take as a native English speaker when "he" is used to talk about a woman. "That can't be?!"

Taylor: Well now you know why.

Nunn: I and other writers use postcolonial theory in talking about your work. But I'm more aware now than I was when I wrote the article in this collection that that's not necessarily a good fit. I've encountered a variety of negative reactions from Native writers to the term. Thomas King argues that "post-colonial might be an excellent term to use to describe Canadian literature, but it will not do to describe Native literature." He says the idea of postcolonial writing assumes that "the struggle between guardian and ward is the catalyst for contemporary Native literature," and hence "cuts us off from our traditions"(12). That is, Native literature has no integrity of its own, but exists solely in relation to the colonizer. Ojibway scholar Kimberly Blaeser says the "insistence on reading Native literature by way of Western literary theory clearly violates its integrity and performs a new act of colonization and conquest" (55). Anita Heiss, an Australian Aboriginal writer, says:

... the term "post-colonialism" is meaningless to Aboriginal people, bearing in mind the political, social and economic status we currently occupy ... there are few, if any Aboriginal Australian writers who agree with or use the term at all, least of all in relation to their writing ... colonisation, as Aboriginal people interpret it, is very much alive ... (226-7)

So when someone like myself slaps the label "post-colonial" on your writing, how do you respond?

Taylor: I don't understand a lot of them. But there's the fact that as Native people we're not postcolonial, we're still colonized. So I don't know if postcolonial interpretation of Native literature is valid.

Nunn: Thomas King agrees with you absolutely, although he says that some of the detailed methods of postcolonial studies seem to be apropos: for example, in the piece I wrote about you ["Hybridity and Mimicry in the Plays of Drew Hayden Taylor"] I said that you're not writing sit-coms, you're writing Native mimicry of sit-coms, that call some of the things about sit-com into question. And that's one of the things that postcolonial theory talks about: mimicry as mockery. *Someday* should be a lovely Christmas special, but it kicks you in the ass.

Taylor: It's like an apple pie with slightly different ingredients.

Nunn: Yeah. Just so. It make you go, hey, wait a minute. This ain't apple pie. It has that reference to apple pie but it's asserting its difference from it. So I see how this is usable, but I also see the problem that Thomas King points to, and you too. That it's easy enough for mainstream Canada to say, "post," but it isn't "post" for indigenous people. It's still very much present.

Taylor: Well, when you deconstruct the word "postcolonial," it makes me think of a log holding up a house, 'cause colonial is a type of architecture too.

Nunn: Thomas King also said that, as soon as you talk about Native literature in terms of postcolonial you're assuming that it starts from the moment of colonization, so it has no connection whatsoever to the whole tradition of storytelling and Native culture.

Taylor: Well, the very fact that all this is in English is indicative of how postcolonial it is. I mean anything that's written in English is by itself altered. Have you ever heard of the Heisenberg principle? Where by observing something you're actually changing it? I think the same principle refers to this.

Nunn: Merely writing in English means you're seeing the world in a sense through somebody else's eyes.

Taylor: Exactly. And even a white person learning to speak an indigenous language much like my mother learning to speak English, it still creates a baffle zone, a level of insulation between its original context and what you've learned to study it.

Nunn: That's right, you can learn to speak it, but you'll still say, "I don't know how they get away without gender, I really don't. I'll do my best."

But I love that phrase from [Armand Garnet] Ruffo's poem about Grey Owl, in which a Native man, knowing that Grey Owl is not Native, yet, speaking for his community, says, "dance with us, as you can"(146). He went about as far as he could go, and he was respected for that, though they knew perfectly well that he'd never make it all the way, he couldn't.

Taylor: The blue eyes were problematic.

Nunn: Well, we've come to the end of my questions. Are any other questions you'd like me to ask or something you'd like to say to end with?

Taylor: The only thing I try and do as a writer, when I'm creating a story, is, I try and create interesting characters, and have an interesting story to tell that takes the audience on an interesting journey. That is basically what I do. So all this postcolonial, postmodern, deconstruction stuff means very little to me. 'Cause I view myself as a contemporary storyteller. And my only function is to go out and have a good time with what I'm doing and tell some really interesting and enjoyable stories that people like and appreciate.

Nunn: So if I catch you right, the "contemporary" is where you are now, the "storyteller" is where you've come from.

Taylor: Yes. It's a highway. With destinations.

Works Cited

Blaeser, Kimberly. "Native Literature: Seeking a Critical Center." *Looking at the Words of Our People: First Nations Analysis of Literature*. Ed. Jeannette Armstrong. Penticton: Theytus, 1993. 51-62.

Campbell, Maria, trans. *Stories of the Road Allowance People*. Penticton: Theytus, 1995.

Heiss, Anita. "Aboriginal Identity and its Effects on Writing." *(Ad)dressing Our Words: Aboriginal Perspectives on Aboriginal Literatures*. Ed. Armand Garnet Ruffo. Penticton: Theytus, 2001. 205-32.

Johnston, Basil. "One Generation from Extinction." *An Anthology of Canadian Native Literature in English*. 2nd ed. Ed. Daniel David Moses and Terry Goldie. Toronto: Oxford University Press, 1998. 99-104.

King, Thomas. "Godzilla vs. Post-Colonial." *World Literature Written in English* 30,2 (1990). 10-16.

Nunn, Robert. "Hybridity and Mimicry in the Plays of Drew Hayden Taylor." *Essays on Canadian Writing* 65 (Fall 1998): 95-119.

Ruffo, Armand Garnet. *Grey Owl: The Mystery of Archie Belaney*. Regina: Coteau, 1996.

Taylor, Drew Hayden. *Further Adventures of a Blue-Eyed Ojibway: Funny, You Don't Look Like One Two*. Penticton: Theytus, 1999.

———. dir. *Redskins, Tricksters and Puppy Stew*. Videocassette. National Film Board of Canada, 2000.

———. *Futile Observations of a Blue-Eyed Ojibway: Funny, You Don't Look Like One, # 4*. Penticton: Theytus, 2004.

Biography of Drew Hayden Taylor

Drew Hayden Taylor was born in 1962 on the Curve Lake First Nation, near Peterborough, Ontario. He was raised on the reserve by his Ojibway mother. He has never known his father, a white man. He has lived in Toronto since 1980, but returns regularly to the reserve to visit family and friends and "recharge his humour batteries." In 1982 he graduated from Seneca College, Toronto, with a diploma in Radio and Television Broadcasting. After graduating, he worked in several media. In radio he worked as Native Affairs reporter for the CBC. In print journalism he contributed articles to a large number of magazines and newspapers, an activity which continues to this day. In television he worked as a consultant on several series, and wrote scripts for "The Beachcombers," "Street Legal," and "North of Sixty." Although he continues to work occasionally in radio and television, his main activity since 1989 has been playwriting. He learned the craft of playwriting during his two-year involvement with the Native theatre company, the De-Ba-Jeh-Mu-Jig Theatre Group, on the Wikwemikong Unceded Reserve, Manitoulin Island, Ontario, from 1989 to 1991, under the mentorship of the director Larry Lewis. He has also had a long association with Canada's premier urban Native theatre company, Native Earth Performing Arts Inc., serving as playwright-in-residence from 1988 to 1989, and as its artistic director from 1994 to 1997. He was also playwright-in-residence with Cahoots Theatre from 2000 to 2001. His plays have been widely produced in Canada, the United States, Germany and Italy. They have received several awards: in 1989, *Toronto at Dreamer's Rock* won the Chalmers Award for best play for young audiences; in 1990, *The Bootlegger Blues* won the Canadian Authors' Association Literary Award for best drama; in 1996, he received the Dora Mavor Moore Award for *Only Drunks and Children Tell the Truth;* he has received the Native Playwrights Award, sponsored by the University of Alaska, Anchorage, twice: in 1996 for *The Baby Blues,* and in 1997 for *Pranks* (now titled *alterNatives*). Also in 1997 he received the James Buller Award for Best Playwright presented by the Centre for Indigenous Theatre. In 2002 he was awarded the Siminovitch Prize in Theatre for *alterNatives.* Many of his plays are in print. In addition, he has published *Fearless Warriors,* a collection of short stories, and four collections of his journalistic writings under the running title *Funny, You Don't Look Like One.* He has travelled widely, lecturing on Native theatre in Canada at conferences in Mexico, Germany, France, Belgium, Italy, India, Australia, New Zealand and

Finland, running workshops in Canada and the United States, and reading from his work at authors' festivals, including the International Festival of Authors, Harbourfront, Toronto. Since 1997 he has organized the Whetung Storyteller's Festival and the Whetung Music Festival at the Curve Lake First Nation. In 2004 he was appointed by the Ministry of Culture of the Government of Ontario to the Minister's Advisory Council for Arts and Culture.

Bibliography

STAGE PLAYS:
(Particulars of first performance are followed by those of publication)

Taylor, Drew Hayden. *Toronto at Dreamer's Rock*. De-Ba-Jeh-Mu-Jig Theatre Group, Sheshegwaning Reserve, Manitoulin Island, Ontario, October 3, 1989. *Toronto at Dreamer's Rock* and *Education Is Our Right: Two One-Act Plays*. Saskatoon: Fifth House, 1990. *Toronto at Dreamer's Rock*. Ed. Albert Reiner Glaap. Berlin: Cornelsen, 1995.

———. *The Bootlegger Blues*. De-Ba-Jeh-Mu-Jig Theatre Group, Wikwemikong Unceded Reserve, Manitoulin Island, Ontario, August 2, 1990. Saskatoon: Fifth House, 1991.

———. *Education Is Our Right*. De-Ba-Jeh-Mu-Jig Theatre Group, East Main, Quebec, February 4, 1990. *Toronto at Dreamer's Rock* and *Education Is Our Right: Two One-Act Plays*. Saskatoon: Fifth House, 1990.

———. *Talking Pictures*. De-Ba-Jeh-Mu-Jig Theatre Group, Wikwemikong Unceded Reserve, Manitoulin Island, Ontario, 1990. Unpublished.

———. *A Contemporary Gothic Indian Vampire Story*. Persephone Theatre, Saskatoon, Saskatchewan, 1992. Unpublished.

———. *Someday*. De-Ba-Jeh-Mu-Jig Theatre Group, Wikwemikong Unceded Reserve, Manitoulin Island, Ontario, November 4, 1991. Saskatoon: Fifth House, 1993.

———. *The All Complete Aboriginal Show Extravaganza*. Youtheatre, 1994. Unpublished.

———. *The Baby Blues*. Arbour Theatre, Peterborough, Ontario, February 17, 1995. Vancouver: Talonbooks, 1999.

———. *Only Drunks and Children Tell the Truth*. Native Earth Performing Arts, Native Canadian Centre, Toronto, Ontario, April 2, 1996. Vancouver: Talonbooks, 1998.

———. *alterNatives*. Bluewater Summer Playhouse, Kincardine, Ontario, July 21, 1999. Vancouver: Talonbooks, 2000.

———. *Girl Who Loved Her Horses*. Theatre Direct, Toronto, Ontario, May 24, 1995. *The Boy in the Treehouse* and *Girl Who Loved Her Horses*. Vancouver: Talonbooks, 1995. "Girl Who Loved Her Horses: A One-Act Play for Young Audiences." *The Drama Review* 41.3 (1997): 153–81.

———. *The Boy in the Treehouse*. Manitoba Theatre for Young People, Winnipeg, Manitoba, May 11, 2000 (tour). *The Boy in the Treehouse* and *Girl Who Loved Her Horses*. Vancouver: Talonbooks, 1995.

———. *400 Kilometres*. Two Planks and a Passion Theatre, Nova Scotia and New Brunswick, March, 1999. Vancouver: Talonbooks, 2005.

———. *Toronto@Dreamer'sRock.com*. De-Ba-Jeh-Mu-Jig Theatre Group, Wikwemikong Unceded Reserve, Manitoulin Island, Ontario, June 28, 1999. Unpublished.

———. *Sucker Falls: A Musical About Demons of the Forest and the Soul*. Touchstone Theatre, Vancouver, B.C., 2001. Adapt. of The Rise and Fall of the City of Mahagonny by Bertolt Brecht. Unpublished.

———. *The Buz'Gem Blues*. Lighthouse Theatre, Port Dover, Ontario, July 5, 2001. Vancouver: Talonbooks, 2002.

———. *Indian Time*. Writ. in collaboration with the 2004 Circle of Voices Program participants. Saskatchewan Native Theatre Company, Saskatoon, Saskatchewan, March 26, 2004. Unpublished.

———. *Raven Stole the Sun*. Red Sky Performance, Milk International Children's Festival of the Arts, Harbourfront, Toronto, Ontario, May 23, 2004. Unpublished.

———. *In a World Created by a Drunken God*. Persephone Theatre, Saskatoon, Saskatchewan, December 2, 2004. Vancouver: Talonbooks, 2006.

OTHER PUBLICATIONS

Nolan, Yvette, Betty Quan, and George Bwanika Seremba. *Beyond the Pale: Dramatic Writing from First Nations Writers and Writers of Colour.* Toronto: Playwrights Canada Press, 1996. Excerpt from *Someday,* 16-27.

Taylor, Drew Hayden and Linda Jaine, ed. *Voices: Being Native in Canada.* Saskatoon: University of Saskatchewan Press, 1992. Includes the short story, "Girl Who Loved Her Horses."

Taylor, Drew Hayden. "Alive and Well: Native Theatre In Canada." *Journal of Canadian Studies* 31.3 (1996): 29-37. Rpt. in American Indian Theater in Performance: A Reader. Edited by Hanay Geiogamah and Jaye T. Darby, American Indian Studies Center Publications, UCLA, 2000.

———. *Funny, You Don't Look Like One: Observations from a Blue-Eyed Ojibway.* Penticton: Theytus, 1996. Rev. ed. Penticton: Theytus, 1998.

———. "The Re-Appearance of the Trickster: Native Theatre in Canada." *On-Stage and Off-Stage: English Canadian Drama in Discourse.* Ed. Albert-Reiner Glaap and Rolf Althof. St. John's: Breakwater, 1996. 51-59.

———. "Storytelling to Stage: The Growth of Native Theatre in Canada." *The Drama Review* 41.3 (1997): 140-52.

———. *Fearless Warriors.* Vancouver: Talonbooks, 1998. Short stories.

———. "Pretty Like a White Boy: The Adventures of a Blue-Eyed Ojibway." *An Anthology of Canadian Native Literature in English.* 2nd ed. Ed. Daniel David Moses and Terry Goldie. Toronto: Oxford University Press, 1998. 436-39. Rpt. from *Funny, You Don't Look Like One: Observations from a Blue-Eyed Ojibway,* 1st ed. 9-14.

———. *Further Adventures of a Blue-Eyed Ojibway: Funny, You Don't Look Like One Two.* Penticton: Theytus, 1999.

——. *Furious Observations of a Blue-Eyed Ojibway: Funny, You Don't Look Like One Two Three*. Penticton: Theytus, 2002.

——. "Canoeing the Rivers of Canadian Aboriginal Theatre: The Portages and the Pitfalls." *Crucible of Cultures: Anglophone Drama at the Dawn of a New Millennium*. Ed. Marc Maufort and Franca Bellarsi. Brussels: Peter Lang, 2002. 25-30.

——. *Futile Observations of a Blue-Eyed Ojibway: Funny, You Don't Look Like One,* # 4. Penticton: Theytus, 2004.

——. "A Blurry Image on the Six O'Clock News." Short story. *Our Story: Aboriginal Voices on Canada's Past*. Toronto: Doubleday Canada, 2004. 220-43.

TELEVISION AND RADIO WRITING
Television

Taylor, Drew Hayden, writ. "A House Divided." *The Beachcombers*. CBC, 1988.

——. writ. "In Search of a Dream." *Street Legal*. CBC, 1989.

——. writ. "All About Leslie." *North of Sixty*. CBC, 1992. (Banff Festival Series Finalist.)

——. writ. "Injuns Amongst Us." *30 second and 2 minute Public Service Announcements*. Centre For Aboriginal Media, 1999. Rpt. in *Futile Observations of a Blue-Eyed Ojibway*, 135 -37.

——. writ. "Prairie Berry Pie." *Access*. The Knowledge Network and TVO, 2000.

——. dir. *Redskins, Tricksters and Puppy Stew*. Videocassette. National Film Board of Canada, 2000.

——. writ. *The Strange Case of Bunny Weequod*. CBC, 2000. (All dialogue in Ojibway.)

——. writ. "The Stuff Dreams Are Made Of" and "Momma and Poppa." *The Longhouse Tales*. Perf. Tom Jackson. CBC/TVO, 2000.

———. writ. "Opening monologues." *Buffalo Tracks*. Prod. Gary Farmer. Aboriginal Peoples Television Network, 2002. Celebrity talk show. Single monologue rpt. in *Futile Observations of a Blue-Eyed Ojibway,* 148-49.

———. writ. and dir. *The Circle of All Nations*. Aboriginal Peoples Television Network, April 25, 2002.

Radio

Drew Hayden Taylor, writ. Episode of Booster McCrane. *Morningside*. CBC, 1993.

———. writ. *Toronto at Dreamer's Rock*. German trans. Albert-Reiner Glaap. Westdeutsche Rundfunk, Nov. 1, 1996.

———. writ. Three stories. *Between the Covers*. CBC, 1999. From *Fearless Warriors*.

———. writ. "Ice Screams." *Sunday Showcase/Monday Night Playhouse*. CBC, January 24-25, 2004. Adapt. from "Ice Screams" in *Fearless Warriors*.

———. writ. "A Blurry Image on the Six O'clock News." *Between the Covers*. CBC, 2005. From *Our Stories: Aboriginal Voices on Canada's Past*.

CRITICAL ARTICLES AND INTERVIEWS

Appleford, Robert. "The Indian 'Act': Postmodern Perspectives on Native Canadian Theatre." Diss. University of Toronto, 1999. 144-191.

Däwes, Birgit. "Local or Global? Negotiations of Identity in Drew Hayden Taylor's Plays." *Global Challenges and Regional Responses in Contemporary Drama in English*. Contemporary Drama in English 10. Ed. Jochen Achilles, Ina Bergmann and Birgit Däwes. Trier: Wissenschaftlicher Verlag Trier, 2002. 217-231.

———. "An Interview with Drew Hayden Taylor." *Contemporary Literature* 44.1 (Spring 2003), 1-18.

Dewar, Jonathan R. "From Copper Woman to Grey Owl to the alterNative Warrior: Exploring Voice and the Need to Connect." *(Ad)dressing Our Words: Aboriginal Perspectives on Aboriginal Literatures.* Ed. Armand Garnet Ruffo. Penticton: Theytus, 2001. 57-77.

Glaap, Albert Reiner. "Diversity in Native Cultures: A Conversation with Drew Hayden Taylor and Dawn T. Maracle." *Zeitschrift für Kanada-Studien* 1999/19. Jg./Nr.1/Bd. 35.

———. "Drew Hayden Taylor's Dramatic Career." *Siting the Other: Revisions of Marginality in Australian and Canadian Drama.* Ed. Marc Maufort and Franca Bellarsi. Brussels: P.I.E. Peter Lang, 2001. 217-232.

———. "Margo Kane, Daniel David Moses, Yvette Nolan, Drew Hayden Taylor: Four Native Playwrights from Canada: An Interview." *Anglistik: Mitteilungen des Verbandes Deutscher Anglisten* 7.1 (1996): 5-25.

———. "New Voices in Canada: Contemporary Plays by Three First Nations Authors." *What Revels are in Hand? Assessments of Contemporary Drama in English in Honour of Wolfgang Lippke.* Eds. Bernhard Reitz and Heiko Stahl. CDE Studies 8. Trier: Wissenschaftlicher Verlag Trier, 2001. 227-237.

———. "*Someday:* Drew Hayden Taylor." *Voices from Canada: Focus on Thirty Plays.* Ed. Albert-Reiner Glaap. Trans. from German by Nicholas Quaintmere. Toronto: Playwrights Canada, 2003. 92-95.

Goldie, Terry. "Interview With Daniel David Moses and Drew Hayden Taylor." *Open Letter* 8.8 (1994): 41-51.

Knowles, Ric and Monique Mojica. "Introduction to Girl Who Loved Her Horses." *Staging Coyote's Dream: An Anthology of First Nations Drama in English.* Ed. Monique Mojica and Ric Knowles. Toronto: Playwrights Canada, 2003. 313-14.

Maufort, Marc. "Drew Hayden Taylor's Alternative Playwriting." *Transgressive Itineraries: Postcolonial Hybridizations of Dramatic Realism.* Brussels: P. I. E. Peter Lang, 2003. 164-76.

———. "Forging an 'Aboriginal Realism': First Nations Playwriting in Australia and Canada." *Siting the Other: Revisions of Marginality in Australian and Canadian Drama*. Ed. Marc Maufort and Franca Bellarsi. Brussels: P.I.E. Peter Lang, 2001. 722.

Moffat, John and Sandy Tait. "Interview with Drew Hayden Taylor." *Canadian Literature* 183 (Winter 2004): 72-86.

Nunn, Robert. "Drew Hayden Taylor's *alterNatives*: Dishing the Dirt." *Crucible of Cultures: Anglophone Drama at the Dawn of a New Millennium*. Eds. Marc Maufort & Franca Bellarsi. Brussels: P. I. E. Peter Lang, 2002. 209-218.

———. "Hybridity and Mimicry in the Plays of Drew Hayden Taylor." *Essays on Canadian Writing* 65 (Fall 1998): 95-119. Rpt. in Aboriginal Drama and Theatre. Ed. Rob Appleford. Toronto: Playwrights Canada, 2005. 74-94.

Ziaja-Buchholtz, Miroslava. "Native Boy's Bluest Eye: Drew Hayden Taylor and Jordan Wheeler Between Politics and Myth." *Canadian Children's Literature/Littérature canadienne pour la jeunesse* 105-106 (Spring-Summer 2002), 114-125.

Selected Reviews

"Awasikan's Bootlegger Blues." Rev. of *The Bootlegger Blues*. *Weetamah,* March 12, 1991.

Bailey, Andrew. "Lighthouse Theatre's "Bootlegger Blues" is a sure cure for the summertime blues." Rev. of *The Bootlegger Blues. Port Dover Maple Leaf,* June 30, 1993.

Birnie, Peter. "Two cultures meet, often hilariously." Rev. of *Only Drunks and Children Tell the Truth. Vancouver Sun,* January 19, 1998.

Casper, Michael. "Play mixes British theatre, Native American culture." Rev. of *The Baby Blues. Altoona Mirror,* July 10, 1990.

Chapman, Geoff. "Large helpings of humor make the pain palatable." Rev. of *Someday. Toronto Star,* November 20, 1994: C6.

Coulbourn, John. "Sometimes, you just have to laugh." Rev. of *The Baby Blues. Toronto Sun,* November 15, 1997: 37.

Crook, Barbara. "Someday you might consider seeing this fine play." Rev. of *Someday. Vancouver Sun,* November 21, 1995.

Donnelly, Pat. "Someday is bittersweet gem." Rev. of *Someday. Montreal Gazette,* October 29, 1994.: D5.

Doruyter, Renee. "Grim idea, good effort." Rev. of *Someday. Vancouver Province,* November 28, 1995: B4.

Fuller, Cam. "Simon's vision quest thoughtful, entertaining." Rev. of *The Boy in the Treehouse. Saskatoon StarPhoenix,* June 3, 2000.

——. "Two Actors Meet Demands of New Play." Rev. of *In a World Created by a Drunken God. Saskatoon StarPhoenix,* Dec. 6, 2004: B2.

Harrison, Riva. "Toronto tackles heady issues with hip humor." Rev. of *Toronto at Dreamer's Rock. Winnipeg Sun,* February 22, 1997: 16.

Kosterski, Laura. "At home on the range." Rev. of *Someday. Eye,* November 24, 1994.

Ledingham, Jo. "Humorous Drunks tells honest story." Rev. of *Only Drunks and Children Tell the Truth. Vancouver Courier,* February 23, 1997: 19-20.

——. "Someday a sober comedy." Rev. of *Someday. Vancouver Courier,* November 22, 1995: 19.

Martindale, Sheila. "*Toronto at Dreamer's Rock:* Tough Issues and Glimmers of Understanding." Rev. of *Toronto at Dreamer's Rock. Scene,* November 23-29, 1995.

Matyas, Joe. "Cast shines in intimate space." Rev. of *Toronto at Dreamer's Rock. London Free Press,* November 12, 1995: C3.

Minogue, Sarah. "On stage: AlterNatives serves up cross-cultural confection." *Nunatsiaq News,* July 9, 2004.

Nicholls, Liz. "Being young + native = alienation." Rev. of *Toronto at Dreamer's Rock. Edmonton Journal,* November 22, 1996. C6.

Peterson, Brian. "Someday soon." Rev. of *Someday*. *Kitsilano News,* November 22, 1995: 32.

Prokosh, Kevin. "MYTP's Boy in the Treehouse achieves lofty goal." Rev. of *The Boy in the Treehouse*. *Winnipeg Free Press,* May 14, 2000.

——— . "Native play fun and encouraging." Rev. of *Toronto at Dreamer's Rock*. *Winnipeg Free Press,* February 21, 1997.

Taylor, Kate. "An identity crisis without reasons." Rev. of *Only Drunks and Children Tell the Truth*. *Globe and Mail,* April 8, 1996: C3.

———. "Heavy issues in light but likable drama." Rev. of *Someday*. *Globe and Mail,* November 22, 1994: C3.

———. "Life on the reserve as a TV sitcom." Rev. of *The Baby Blues*. *Globe and Mail,* November 18, 1997: C3.

Thomas, Colin. "Tell the Truth." Rev. of *Only Drunks and Children Tell the Truth*. *Georgia Straight,* February 20, 1997.

———. *"The Buz'Gem Blues."* Rev. *Georgia Straight,* April 8, 2004.

Todd, Rebecca. *"The Baby Blues."* Rev. of *The Baby Blues*. *Eye,* November 20, 1997: 42.

Wagner, Vit. "Dancing fast as he can." Rev. of *The Baby Blues*. *Toronto Star,* November 16, 1997: B3.

———. "Two plays look deeply into Indians' hearts." Rev. of *Toronto at Dreamer's Rock*. *Toronto Star,* January 27, 1991: H6.

Wilkinson, Steve. "Audience laughs away the Blues." Rev. of *The Baby Blues*. *Peterborough Examiner,* February 25, 1995.

Contributors

Rob Appleford is an Associate Professor in the English and Film Studies Department at the University of Alberta. He teaches and researches in the areas of Canadian Aboriginal/First Nations Literatures and Native American Literatures, with an emphasis on contemporary and emergent writing and critical theory. He has edited a collection of essays on Canadian Aboriginal Drama and Theatre for Playwrights Canada Press (2005). Currently, he is at work on a book-length study of desire and Aboriginal identity formation entitled *The Politics of Desire in North American Aboriginal Literatures*.

Birgit Däwes received her M.A. degree from the University of Mainz in 2000 and teaches American Literature and Culture at the University of Würzburg, Germany. Her publications focus on Native American and First Nations literatures, issues of globalization and cultural memory, as well as contemporary American fiction and film; including a recently co-edited volume on *Global Challenges and Regional Responses in Contemporary Drama in English*. She is currently completing a Ph.D. thesis on Native North American Theatre.

Jonathan Dewar is Director of the Métis Centre of the National Aboriginal Health Organization. He was formerly senior communications advisor to the Intergovernmental Affairs and Inuit Relations Directorate with Indian and Northern Affairs Canada's Nunavut regional office. While living in Iqaluit he was a founding member and executive director of the Qaggiq Theatre Company, an Iqaluit-based literary and performing arts organization that works with youth on Inuit cultural and social issues. A former SSHRC doctoral fellow, Jonathan's research took him to Nunavut in 2001. As a person of mixed heritage (Huron-Wendat/Métis and Scottish/French Canadian), Jonathan Dewar is interested in explorations of culture and identity.

Kristina Fagan is a member of the Labrador Métis Nation and grew up in St. John's, Newfoundland. After completing her Ph.D. at the University of Toronto in 2001, she joined the English Department at the University of Saskatchewan where she teaches Aboriginal literature. Her research interests include the role of humour in Aboriginal literature and the relationship between oral and written traditions.

Ric Knowles is Professor of Theatre at the University of Guelph and editor of *Canadian Theatre Review*. His most recent book is *Reading the Material Theatre,* published by Cambridge University Press in 2004.

Monique Mojica, actor and published playwright, belongs to the second generation spun from the web of New York's Spiderwoman Theater. A veteran theatre artist and former Artistic Director of Native Earth Performing Arts, she is 1/3 of Turtle Gals Performance Ensemble, which she co-founded with Jani Lauzon and Michelle St. John.

Robert Nunn taught dramatic literature and theatre history and theory at Brock University until his retirement in 2000. He has published numerous essays on Canadian plays and playwrights, including Hrant Alianak, David Fennario, David French, Sharon Pollock, Judith Thompson, and Drew Hayden Taylor. Two of his essays were awarded the Richard Plant Essay Prize. He was co-editor of *Theatre Research in Canada/Recherches théâtrales au Canada* from 1993 to 1996, and is on the editorial board of that journal as well as *Essays in Theatre/Études théâtrales*.